Confidence Formula (Workbook)

How to attain a Bulletproof Self-Esteem & Master Stress Reduction Even If You've Never Felt Any

Alex Wallace

omissions, or inaccuracies.

Table of Contents

Introduction

We live in a world that is more judgmental than ever before. There never seems to be the right kind of person. You might be the most hilarious person that most have encountered, but there will always be a decent-sized crowd that doesn't understand your jokes.

Anyone can get online and find some fragments of information about you. Even if you try to actively stay off social media, you could still end up in someone else's profile through group photos. All of these moments of exposure open us up to judgments and criticism from other people.

It's clear that the judgment will never stop. That doesn't mean we have to skip out on moments in life that we love just because we're afraid of what other people might think of us. You deserve to feel comfortable in your own skin and unafraid to be authentically yourself.

Someone is always going to make you feel insecure, whether intentional or not. These moments of vulnerability shouldn't be validations to keep ourselves hidden away. Even if we're not intentionally hiding our bodies through the clothes we wear or the way we crop photos, it's easy to hide your personality. When you're talking to someone directly, you might still have moments of inauthenticity, holding back your feelings or putting on a fake expression to hide an emotion. This can be draining if we have to do it repeatedly.

Unlock the masks you've been hiding behind and free yourself from the chains that have kept you bound to a persona that doesn't reflect who you truly are.

It's easy to realize we need to build our confidence, but the hard part is practically doing it.

You might struggle to know how to overcome these constant fears because of what you're told to help remedy them. Some will say, "Who cares what other people think?" and remind you to "just be yourself!"

Yes, of course, these things are important. But how do we actually cultivate this mindset? After years of being told that we are not good enough, smart enough, funny enough, attractive enough, successful enough, and everything in between, what can a person do to help themselves out of the deep pit self-hate has created?

The solution to this endless despair is to include practical exercises in your life on a daily basis to help you overcome constant negative feelings.

In this book, we have provided over 30 practical exercises for you to overcome these feelings. They include everything from simple mental exercises to daily routines for a healthier and happier life.

Confidence is everything. It is required for most aspects of your life. It's not something that can simply be faked all the time. Faking it might help in the beginning, but eventually, things fall through if you're not being true to yourself.

Confidence gives you the motivation to push forward. It's a reminder that you can achieve what you hope to if you actively strive to reach your goals. It's a validation that you are strong enough to work through the most terrifying situations. Confidence is necessary to keep you surviving and prospering in our fast-paced world.

Your brain has developed to become exactly what it is now. Every experience you've lived through was one notch in the knowledge you've acquired now. Often, we let these things become negative reminders of the past guilty feelings and resentful emotions. By changing the way you think now and altering mental habits, it's easier to increase your emotional.

If you can look back on your life and truly make the most of every situation, it will help enable you to propel towards the success you deserve.

Research shows that you can restructure your brain through repetitive mental exercises.

Cognitive fitness is essential for achieving more complex neurological functions in your brain. Instead of struggling with anxious thoughts and constant self-doubt, you can challenge your brain to become more mentally fit (Gilkey & Kilts, 2007).

One of the biggest benefits of increased confidence is to have the ability to reduce stress. Wondering if other people like you, worrying about the thoughts and opinions of others, and constantly doubting yourself can take a toll on every aspect of your life. You might struggle with your ability to process information and pay attention. It could be challenging to focus and stand up for yourself as needed.

Confidence will benefit your life by increasing your ability to enjoy a moment. Rather than stressing over what you're going to wear at a party, you'll be able to actually enjoy the moments you're there. Instead of worrying about how you're going to pay your bills all the time, you'll come up with more effective financial solutions after clearing your head.

Confidence can be contagious. If you have children, a spouse with low self-esteem, or just the people you hang around with in general, you can have great effects on the way they see themselves as well.

We all deserve to cultivate this kind of happiness in our life. It's something real and achievable, and it's done so through applying yourself to these methods.

Many of these activities are inclusive of cognitive behavioral therapy (CBT). This is a method that has helped countless people achieve freedom from constant anxiety or depression. Almost all of these treatments and practical exercises have research that supports their legitimacy.

Of course, we are all different. Perhaps you've tried CBT methods in the past and they haven't worked for you. Maybe you're sick of journaling and have never found use from it. That's fine!

We have taken these methods and put a new twist on them for more engagement and satisfaction. There are plenty of regurgitated bits of advice and cheesy exercises that no one actually enjoys doing.

This book will leave you feeling refreshed and rejuvenated at the end with a brand-new confident spirit. You deserve to live an exciting life, and that can be done by navigating through this workbook.

The structure includes background information to give you a better understanding of the subject with practical exercises to follow. Go at your own pace and never push yourself to do anything you're uncomfortable with if you're not ready. We are all different with complex experiences and backgrounds that make us entirely unique. What is someone else's medicine might not be yours, so it's OK to give some exercises more attention than others.

The point is to boost your confidence to help you excel in all areas of life. Don't wait for this moment to come to you. You are the one in charge of your own perception, and no one else will be able to fulfill that role. Increase your esteem and overcome issues with confidence by taking the first step: coming up with a crystal-clear plan.

Chapter 1: Crystal-Clear Plan

Before diving into this, it's going to be beneficial for you to come up with a clear goal and idea for what you hope to gain at the end. Before setting goals for major life milestones — the career, spouse, dream body — focus on creating goals for how you hope to become more confident.

Goals are essential for helping us have an idea of what to do next. They create the structure for how we are going to continue to propel into the future. Whenever you have a goal, they can be the basis of judgment for whether or not you should do something. Ask yourself if it would align with the vision you have in the future to know if it is something that's good for you now.

Goal setting seems easy, but that's not always the case. Once you've understood how to come up with goals for who you want to be, you can create goals for what you want to do.

What Kind of Confidence Do You Want?

There are different kinds of confidence that you can develop over time. One of the most important kinds of confidence is self-confidence. Are you able to trust in your own abilities, and do you recognize that you are in control of a situation?

You have the power, and it's your abilities that make you the successful individual you are.

You also want to recognize knowing how to stand up for yourself and how to take charge of a situation. How do you ask for what you need and control what you have power over?

Can you be an independent person who doesn't rely on any external circumstances to provide you with that deep inner value? Are you able to cultivate these feelings on your own? These are all-inclusive in an individual that has a high level of self-confidence. This area might be lacking in your life if you feel as though you have no ability to trust in yourself.

It's also important to recognize your ability to have confidence in other people. Sometimes we need so much control that it's hard to give that power to others. We might be feeling insecure about ourselves. We might not have that intention or purpose, and maybe we're gliding through only by controlling others.

This can leave us not having faith in individuals that deserve it.

Perhaps you struggled to let yourself be vulnerable in front of other people. It's hard to connect with someone when you don't have the confidence that they are able to understand where you are coming from. It's easy to shut people out like this, especially when so many might have let us down in the past.

Maybe you like to put on the façade that you're a strong person, but really you break down frequently and struggle with your emotions because it is so challenging for you to open up. This can leave us lacking confidence. Though it might seem like that strong hard outer shell does show independence, you could be lacking that emotional control inside.

By putting confidence in other people, you're able to recognize individuality. You appreciate some of the things that might be seen as flaws because you respect the originality that everybody has. If you lack confidence with other people, you might question their intelligence. Maybe you're going out of town, and you tell everyone at home a million times what they have to do when they're gone. Perhaps you remind your roommate too often to water the plants, or you constantly check in with your spouse to make sure they remembered to feed and bathe the kids.

Some individuals lack confidence in what others say. Do you find yourself ever making up for someone else's embarrassing moments or mistakes in a conversation? Perhaps you worry others will be offended by their joke, so you feel the need to add, "That's just the way he is!" or, "It's just his personality," in different situations.

You might often lack confidence in someone else's ability to take care of themselves. Perhaps you go out of your way to provide them with help or aid when they don't need it. You could even be too much of a mediator between friends or family members to the point that you drive a deeper wedge between the two. Lacking confidence in other people affects not only you but also those that you struggle to give faith to.

You can have a lack of confidence in the future. Sometimes we don't trust in all that is going to be coming our way. We struggle to have faith over things turning out in our favor.

Lacking this faith can leave us feeling very negative and lacking hope. It's hard to care about doing anything at all if you're not excited about what will occur in the future.

Perhaps you struggled to ever have any good feelings about the future. If you've lived through a lot of negative experiences or struggle with chronic anxiety, it's likely challenging for you to have any hope for good things happening.

This can end up leaving you feeling like there's no point in continuing on. Why wake up in the morning and begin to accomplish goals if everything's just going to turn out bad? This kind of confidence is really struggling.

Out of these areas that you can have confidence in your life, where do you think you're struggling now?

If you're looking at what you want to improve on, do you think it's lies within you, or do you think it's part of your perspective that you carry about other people? Is it deeper confidence you're seeking or something in the way you interact with those around you?

How can you begin to change these things or confront them as they occur to help you get over the constant doubt or fear?

Setting your goals is the first process when developing greater confidence.

The Importance of Goals

Goals are important because they provide you with confidence. One of the key elements of goal setting is wanting to take care of your future self.

By making that effort towards wanting to have a better future, you're giving yourself the opportunity to create responsible habits. When you have a goal, you have to break it down in a realistic way. You have to come up with something that you can actually achieve and a goal that you know is possible based on your strengths. Goal setting involves a lot of reflection. Each time you hit one of those goals, you give yourself a little boost of confidence.

Let's say your goal is to lose 20 pounds. You could wait until the end of it all to hop on the scale and see that you've lost that 20 pounds. But before that, you're going to notice little milestones.

Maybe you start to fit in clothes better. Perhaps you have more energy from working out. There are little rewards along the way that keep your self-esteem at a consistently high level.

Each of those is going to boost your self-esteem and remind you that you are a strong and capable person. You do have the ability to do something good for yourself. You'll look back on time, and you won't have that regret or remorse. You'll recognize that you did what you could to achieve your goals. When you do have a failure or a moment when you don't achieve a goal, it's another opportunity to reflect. You take the time to look at what you could have done better and discover new ways to improve.

It's a great way to have a good feeling all the time. When something doesn't go right or if you have a bad day, you can still remind yourself of your success based on how you've been keeping track of your goals.

We need tasks. We are very intelligent animals that recognize we should be serving a purpose. It provides us with clarity and concentration. It fulfills us and makes us recognize our individual abilities. We become aware of the benefits that we have to offer those around us.

We see the value that exists in ourselves, and that helps us feel good often. Setting goals is going to be your way of really taking care of yourself. It increases confidence because you trust in your abilities. You give yourself these challenging things to overcome, and you recognize your ability to follow through with that.

When you set goals, there are going to be moments where you think to yourself, "Hmm, that might be a little too difficult, but I guess I'll try!" Then when you succeed, you're able to impress yourself. After consistently achieving goals, you will feel confident to the point that you are your own role model. There's nothing more fulfilling than being proud of yourself.

By giving yourself solid goals to reach for, you see that you are somebody who has a purpose. You have an intention, you have meaning, and you have a reason.

When you wake up in the morning, you know what you have to do for the day. You see that you have certain tasks that needs to be finished.

Once you complete those, you can look in the mirror and feel confident about yourself. You know that next time there is a problem, you're going to be able to overcome it, just like you did with this.

It's a reminder that lets us see our own personal value. It's the way that we've developed the skills we have now! Life certainly hasn't been easy, but we've overcome the obstacles that have been thrown at us. Now it is time to challenge yourself. Building your confidence is the perfect place to start because it will give you the encouraging reminder that you'll be able to continue on through everything that you might face.

The Keys to Goal Setting

The first step to goal setting is reflecting on why you want to achieve this goal. What is it about the outcome that draws you in? What are you most hoping to achieve from setting out to reach this goal?

You have to be in tune with what you hope to gain for yourself to have the desire to get that. In this process of reflecting, you might discover that it's not actually your goal. Perhaps you've just been made to feel as though you need to achieve this goal throughout your life. For example, many of us are pressured to get a high-paying job to have a fancy house with a family. Maybe some people don't want that. Perhaps you just want to travel with your backpack and truck around the country. Maybe you're more interested in living in a high-rise building as a single, cosmopolitan, independent woman. Whatever you choose is up to you, so come up with the goal that satisfies your needs.

Don't feel like you have to consider every other person. Of course, if you have children or are married, you are going to be more dedicated to them.

However, your goals should still be inclusive of your desires.

It's also important that your goals are possible in the first place. If they're not realistically achievable, you are just setting yourself up for failure from the start.

Don't make the goal to become a millionaire by the end of the year if you are currently over $30,000 in debt. You can't really earn a million dollars in a year if you aren't already in good financial standing. You could win the lottery or become a viral sensation, but we all know we have a better chance of getting into a deeper negative financial situation than either of those. Perhaps you do increase your bank account that much, but usually, there's more of a build-up before that.

You also want to ensure that your goals are things that can be measured. Have them be specific. Don't just say, "I hope to be attractive one day."

Instead, have more specific goals to make you feel more attractive, such as the following:

- Building your confidence by practicing four exercises every week
- Increasing your fitness levels by working out every other day
- Having healthier food by preparing homemade food ahead for the week

You also want to give yourself the opportunity to make sure these goals are things you can fulfill in a certain amount of time.

Have them be realistic.

It's easy to say that you want to be a rich, famous actor who's a millionaire with a business that you own and you're a best-selling author and everything in between.

That's great to have such high goals, but they aren't completely realistic.

There are some people in the world who are like this, but it doesn't happen overnight. Start with one thing that is completely realistic and work your way towards that. Don't center goals on luck. You might be able to become famous easily, but it takes a lot of hard work to do it organically. Plan for that realistic situation rather than banking that you'll win the lottery.

In the meantime, keep it simple and start from there.

Make yourself accountable for achieving these goals. Sometimes this means putting a post online for friends and family to see.

Other moments, it could be investing money into it. Maybe you buy expensive gym equipment for working out. You have to use it so that it doesn't go to waste. That will remind you that you've already made an investment, so now it's time for the payoff.

The last thing to do is set your goal. State that you want to fulfill X goal in Y amount of time. From there, you will draft up your plan for success and begin to get the wheels in motion for victory.

Goal-Setting Exercises

These next three exercises are going to help you better cultivate the necessary skills required to make goal setting a simple part of your life. These three exercises are methods to include in a daily routine. Every morning you wake up or moment before bed is the perfect time to include any of these reflective practices.

Remember to keep an open mind and know that there might be challenging moments. It can be rather frightening to think about some of the haunting moments of our past or times when we felt challenging emotions. It's OK to take small steps to get on the right track towards overcoming mental roadblocks.

The point is to make you feel good about yourself because that is really the key to confidence at the end of the day. You should feel excited about going through your day-to-day activities and not worried about every little thing. The things you are capable of are unstoppable, so enter this process with an open mind and willingness for change.

Visualization

Research shows that the brain won't always know what the difference is between reality and perception (Schacter et al., 2012). In fact, visualizing that you're doing something could be as powerful as actually doing it (Randolph, 2002).

Visualization is a great activity to help you better see what your actual goals are going to look like.

Oftentimes, we fantasize about the things we want in life without fully grasping the reality of everything that might bring along. Visualization is your way of looking at what you hope to gain in the future and seeing if this is a viable option for you. Is it a realistic process that you're actually going to want to live through?

For example, you might really want to be rich and famous one day. Then when you start to visualize, you realize it's not actually one of your desires.

You think you visualize yourself walking to and from just your house to the store with constant paparazzi. Think about all of the people that you might not be able to trust if you were to become wealthy. Are you really the type to give interviews and have that personality, or is it just a fantasy created overtime?

Visualization would involve you going through the day-to-day motions of that future goal. You wouldn't just think of all the great parts that could potentially happen. It requires a realistic evaluation of everything going on.

This is also a way for you to process what might be an issue. If there is a threat or other mishap that wasn't thought about first, going through the process in your mind could potentially help you prevent it from happening.

Visualization is different for imagination because you're going to be looking at the reality of what is going to happen eventually. You're actively taking the opportunity to look through what might happen rather than just creating exciting images in your head.

To start visualization, first, come up with what you plan on creating a goal around. Come up with the idea for what you're going to be striving for soon. Is this something that is your goal, or is it one that's been created for you by other people?

Visualization can just be a mental process that you take time for at the end of your day to journal about the things you're hoping to gain.

You can also visualize in a physical or creative way. You can take pictures and cut them out of magazines, the old-fashioned way, and come up with a vision board. You can also write things down or put them out in public for the world to see. Sometimes this includes simply making a statement online.

To hold yourself accountable, you can share your vision with others and discuss all that's involved to see if there's anything you're missing. Visualization is a great method for you to fully prepare for everything that's going to be coming your way. It'll be easier to notice your flaws and shortcomings and find a way to work through these issues in a healthy way.

Visualize by also remembering that you can ask and talk to people who have first-hand experiences with the same kind of things that you do. The more information and research you can do on your visualization, the easier it is to find a true prediction for what the future holds.

Emotional Tracking Journal

Journaling has numerous health benefits (Purcell, 2018):

- Reducing stress
- Increasing problem-solving skills
- Understanding emotions better

Journaling involves taking your thoughts or feelings and writing them down or sharing them. It involves a reflection from the individual who is journaling. You have likely been told that you should journal before, but we aren't told as frequently *how* to journal.

Journaling is supposed to be an immersive individual experience. So that's what you're going to want to create on your own. How can you take this instance that might have become somewhat pedantic to you at this point and turn it into a legitimate process that will actually help you through?

The first step is to look at journaling outside of the box. It's not taking notes on your life. It's not just writing "Dear diary" entries. It's not drawing doodles and pictures to help express your feelings. It could be these things if that's what you want, but it doesn't have to be.

Journaling can be an analytic and cognitive way to evaluate your emotions. If you're somebody who's a little bit more scientifically structured, you can come up with a way to track your feelings beyond just sketching down in a journal of some sort.

Use a spreadsheet in Excel. Use graph paper to help chart your feelings. You can just use simple symbols. It doesn't always have to be some abstract production.

Start by just journaling once a week. Have a reflection period (maybe on Sundays, Fridays, or even Mondays at the beginning of the week) to help you understand how your emotions might be fluctuating over a time period.

Journaling can also be a very creative process for you if that's what you'd like instead. You could simply take pictures every day and try to remember the emotions that you've attached to those photographs. It doesn't have to be something that is so literal and meaningful. It's not just about sitting there and writing down in a sketch pad. It's not typing away at your computer for hours about your feelings. All of this is perfectly fine if that's what you prefer to do, but it does not have to be that way.

Another great type of journaling is to answer a question or a prompt every day. These kinds of journals have become popular, and you can take this trend and turn it into your own method.

This could include just simply googling emotional reflection questions. You can give yourself daily challenges like looking at quotes and writing about them and how they make you feel.

You can come up with creative stories about your life using exciting storytelling to take a new perspective on experiences you've been through or even just write poetry. You can come up with solid lyrics. You can create sketches and cartoons.

Whatever you choose to do is entirely up to you. You are the one who is in charge of what gets written down or what doesn't. The point is to help you reflect on your emotions so you can better learn what they actually need. Journaling is scientifically proven to help individuals improve their emotional state, so let this be something that helps you dive further into your mind.

Confronting Cognitive Distortions

Cognitive distortions are any thought patterns that prevent you from seeing reality (Grohol, 2019). If you want to set goals, you have to identify what your different cognitive distortions are.

Most of us don't even realize that the patterns of thought we already have are distorted ways of thinking. By recognizing these different mental patterns, it's easier to break them apart so you can overcome their negative effects. The first and most common type of cognitive distortion is polarized thinking. This is also referred to as all-or-nothing thinking. Whenever you have this kind of cognitive distortion, it creates a mental spectrum.

Everything will either fall as being good or bad and nothing else. This kind of thought pattern keeps us trapped in this toxic mentality because we never see anything that is in between. Everything is stuck to either being black or white.

There is no gray area. This causes you to overlook situations that could help enhance your confidence. If you look in the mirror and see that you're having a bad hair day, you can use that to validate your negative perspective on yourself. You tell yourself that you're ugly overall just because your hair looks a little funny.

Recognize this cognitive distortion and replace it by finding the balance. Every time you want to put something on the all-or-nothing spectrum, pick out one thing that can be categorized in the middle.

Another type of cognitive distortion is when we do mind-reading.

This often occurs if you're feeling insecure. After communicating with somebody, you might be waiting for a text back, or maybe you're nervous about an upcoming meeting with your boss. Anytime you try to mind-read and predict what somebody else is thinking, it is a cognitive distortion because we do not have control over other people or the thoughts that they have.

Every time that you try to mind-read, remember to question reality.

Look inwards at yourself and see what the reality of the situation is rather than this hyper-anxious fantasy you started to create.

Absolute phrasing is another type of cognitive distortion. This is anytime you say words like "always," "never," "best," or "worst."

"Can't," "won't," and "should"/"shouldn't" are also words that define something. It fits into polarized thinking because you are instantly labeling a situation by this absolute. You might say, "I never go out on dates with a certain type of guy." Then that type asks you out, and you don't go out with them, missing out on a potential date because of this absolute freeze.

Other kinds of cognitive distortions include the following:

- overgeneralization
- catastrophizing
- personalization

- always being right

Take a moment to reflect, either in your journal or just in your mind, on what cognitive distortions you notice yourself having.

Take a moment to write them down. Each time you notice one, write down what the cognitive distortion is, why it is a disordered pattern of thinking, and what thought you can use to replace it with. You'll eventually have your own catalog of personalized cognitive distortions that will make it easier for you to know how to confront them as they come.

Chapter 2: Self-Esteem, Confidence, and How They Relate

If you look up any interviews with popular celebrities, such as actors and pop stars, you'll likely find many of them struggle with their self-esteem. They might talk about eating disorders or turning to drugs to help them feel better. They seem to have it all, yet they can often continue to struggle with feelings of inadequacy.

How can someone confident enough to get behind a camera and sing or act still not believe in their own abilities? When they have millions of fans who worship them, how can they still struggle with their self-esteem?

It's important to differentiate between self-esteem and confidence. They can go hand in hand, but we need to recognize the difference between the two to nurture both. If you ignore your self-esteem and only focus on confidence, it can sometimes have you trapped in a place of false identity, pretending to be someone you're not.

The Difference Between Self-Esteem and Self-Confidence

Self-esteem and confidence are intertwined with each other in some ways. There's a lot of relation between having high self-esteem and being confident. On the other hand, they also have different qualifications and various aspects that make them separate.

Self-esteem is how you feel on the inside, and confidence can be how you show it. If you do have high self-esteem, sometimes that can be seen, but not everybody shows it in the same way. Confidence doesn't always look alike, and neither does self-esteem. Self-esteem is something that reminds you that you're sure of yourself and that you trust in your own abilities. Self-esteem is like a strong foundation that propels you continually towards a place where you accept your potential.

Confidence can sometimes be the way that you put on a brave face. If you don't have confidence, then your self-esteem can back that up. If you don't have confidence or if you have low self-esteem, then you're going to be really unsure of yourself. For example, think of the way that those pop stars we mentioned might have confidence when they are on stage with makeup on and a crowd of fans. When they're in public around regular people with no makeup and not that huge team backing them up, they might not have that self-esteem to keep them feeling confident.

The confidence came from all the things that were added. However, if they still had that high self-esteem, they could show that by being confident when they're out in public. They might not be afraid to show people their look with no makeup or how their body is presented even if they have imperfections visible.

Self-esteem can be faked. Self-esteem goes deep into yourself. It travels far into how you view yourself and the world around you. Self-esteem is also something that involves other people. Do you believe others admire and respect you, or do you think everybody's making fun of you all the time? Do you have the confidence to know that you are valued and that you have something to offer the world, or do you feel bad about yourself because you think that others hate you all the time? There are different signs of confidence and self-esteem that are also key to remembering.

Is Self-Esteem Natural or Acquired?

Self-esteem can sometimes feel natural. There are people who seem to just have a higher level of confidence. You might envy other people because of their ability to simply not care what others think.

Self-esteem is also something that can be built over time. If you don't have it right now, that doesn't mean that you can't have it in the future. Self-esteem can be acquired through behaviors and attempting to stop bad habits from happening.

As humans, we have different needs that require fulfillment. These needs involve things like feeling safe and feeling loved. We all want that acknowledgment that others value us and the recognition to boost our self-esteem.

It's not that self-esteem is something natural that we have, but it is a natural urge that we have that needs to be fulfilled. Think of it as hunger. It's not a talent like making food. It's simply that feeling and requirement to eat food.

Everybody has this need for self-esteem, and it's fulfilled in different ways. Some people like verbal praise. You might enjoy having other people tell you that they're proud of you.

Other people like attention in romantic ways. They might also value monetary aspects.

That self-esteem can be temporarily fulfilled from other people, external circumstances, and everything in between, but the strongest kind of self-esteem you can build is what is grown within yourself.

Having this natural feeling of confidence is exactly what you need to remind yourself of your abilities. You should feel assured of what you're capable of doing. You want to remind yourself that you have value to offer the world and other people look out for you. You want that urge to be admired and the respect given because it's a natural feeling. It's something that we're all born with. Think about how children enjoy simple praise, like getting stickers for good grades or candy as a reward for behavior.

When we don't have that provided to us throughout our childhood, it can be hard to have that as an adult. Some people who seem to be naturally confident might have just had childhoods that gave them that ability. They might have not had a problem getting the attention they needed for doing things that deserved praise as children.

We will talk further about the experiences that can shape your self-esteem later, but let's dive deeper into what high self-esteem, low self-esteem, high confidence, and low confidence all look like.

Signs of Low Self-Esteem

Low self-esteem can show itself in many different ways. One sign of low self-esteem might be the way that you present yourself. Maybe you often hide behind things. Perhaps you don't show your opinion when asked and, instead, give very general answers. You might feel uncomfortable confronting people when you need to have discussions, and maybe you are even afraid to do things like talking on the phone or messaging people online.

When you have low self-esteem, it might be hard for you to take compliments. You likely don't compliment yourself often, so when somebody else offers that opinion, it's hard for you to accept that as reality. You might wonder if they are messing with you or playing a prank. Having low self-esteem can make us very indecisive. It's challenging to trust in our decisions and know what is right. If you have low self-esteem, you're likely going through all the worst-case scenarios, trying to figure out how that can be prevented by making the perfect decision. That can make us very vulnerable to putting intense pressure on ourselves.

You might not have any motivation if you have low self-esteem. You likely don't believe in yourself or your abilities to complete tasks, and you compare your success with what others have been able to achieve. You think about how you're not as good or talented as somebody else, so why even bother doing anything at all? It can be very defeating to have this kind of constant self-doubt, leaving us trapped in a place where we are afraid of everything. It's exhausting, and anybody who experiences low self-esteem knows they just wish they could believe in themselves.

Signs of Confidence

Having confidence can seem like such a foreign subject to somebody who intensely lacks self-esteem. If you have low confidence, sometimes that can be more about how you present yourself. Perhaps you are fine with being in front of people, and you trust in your abilities, but maybe you still don't have the confidence to get up on stage and perform.

Confident people truly believe in themselves. They don't look for other people to have that validation that they're worth something. Of course, they recognize that having that can provide them with value, but that's not the only thing they based those kinds of feelings off.

Confident people don't doubt their abilities. They recognize they have some weaknesses that likely need to be improved and they aren't perfect; however, they also pay attention to the way that they can fulfill their basic desires and know that they do have a lot of talent because of these powers.

Confident people know how to speak up for what's on their mind. They are able to get the things they know they deserve because of how they operate within a space. Confident people aren't afraid to share their opinion. They know that everybody is different, and they respect the unique distinctions that we have that make us the people we are as individuals.

They respect other people's opinions even when they disagree because they don't need to validate their thoughts and ideas just based on what other people believe.

They are able to solve their own problems or seek help when necessary because they're not afraid to admit that they do have some weaknesses. Confident people are also able to still recognize all the power they possess and the great things they are able to achieve.

Confidence Exercises

Confidence can be built! Even though you might feel cursed, depending on your situation, through practical steps, you'll be able to achieve the unthinkable. We can all benefit from including more confidence-boosting activities in our lives. They aren't just about putting on a fake face and talking with an assertive voice. You should find that inner strength to lift yourself in times when you feel stressed or overwhelmed.

The first activity is to take somewhat of a quiz to know where you are now. It's a method to discover your greatest flaws or shortcomings to focus on the areas that need the most fixing. The second is a mindfulness activity that helps you center yourself no matter what the situation. By including these activities into your life on a daily basis (or even just once a week), you'll notice the difference in your personal ability to believe in your strengths and have courage in your capabilities.

The Self-Esteem Checkup

Below we have a quiz you can take to check in with your self-esteem and where you are at this moment with how you're viewing yourself. The first step in checking your self-esteem is to answer truthfully how you feel internally. Nobody else is going to be checking in with this quiz, so don't exaggerate or understate, depending on what you prefer your perspective to be. Be truthful with your confidence levels, and try to answer the best of your ability.

There are 20 statements below. For each one, rate them from 1 to 5. The scores are as follows:

1 — I don't agree with this whatsoever.

2 — I have felt this way only a few times in my life.

3 — Sometimes I feel like this, but just as often, I feel the opposite.

4 — Most of the time, I feel like this, but there are a few times I don't.

5 — I feel like this pretty much all the time.

Use your best judgment to give a fair score somewhere in between these numbers if you're not sure which one to pick. Keep track because, in the end, we will add them all together to determine your level of self-esteem.

Remember, these are statements that you either agree with or completely disagree with:

1. I am confident in my abilities.
2. I am not afraid of what other people think of me.
3. I do not wait for direction from other people to take action in my life.
4. I am satisfied with the accomplishments that I have made up until now.
5. I never fear that somebody is going to be judging me.
6. I feel as though I am good enough, and I never question my self-worth.
7. I feel like an authentic person, and I am always myself.
8. I am extremely happy with the person I am, and I enjoy being alone.
9. I know how to entertain myself, and it's not uncomfortable when there's nobody else around me.
10. I am not afraid to be alone, and I do not depend on other people.

11. I think people generally enjoy being around me.

12. I don't think about what I said the next day, and I let my feelings of anxiety over a conversation that I've had go.

13. I am not afraid to ask for things when I need them or reach out for help when I know that it is required.

14. I am willing to admit that I am wrong. I reflect on my actions and notice how they hurt other people, so it's not hard for me to tell others I am sorry, and this is something that I actively do often.

15. I am a very intelligent person.

16. No matter what level of knowledge I have, I seek out new information, and I'm excited to learn about different subjects.

17. I never questioned my abilities to complete a task when somebody asks me to.

18. I have many healthy relationships where I feel like communication is open and effective.

19. It's easy for me to accept compliments, and I give compliments to other people often.

20. I rarely criticize myself in a negative way and always know how to improve from what I reflect on.

Now add up all of your scores. The highest possible score is 100 if you got all 5s. The lowest possible score is 20 if you got all 1s.

Anything between 85 and 90 is a great place to be. It shows that you have plenty of confidence and there are just a few instances that take that away.

Anything between 75 and 84 shows that you need to likely improve on your confidence, but the solid foundation is there to do so. This would be a score of mostly 3s or 4s, with maybe a few 5s in there.

Something between 60 and 74 shows that your confidence is pretty low and might be so because of a clear factor. Maybe you're unhappy with your status in life or the way you look.

Anything less than 50 shows that you are struggling with confidence, and you can see that as it gets lower, this is a problem. If you got a solid 20 with every answer being a 1, there is a chance there's an underlying condition affecting your self-esteem, such as anxiety or depression.

Getting a perfect 100 but also seeking out this confidence book might mean that your confidence is misguided. You might be struggling because you can act confident, but you're not actually feeling it deep down.

If all these questions were very easy for you and you believed you had 5 for every single one, then question what it is you think you might be lacking about your confidence. Perhaps you don't have that confidence within yourself, and you didn't answer these truthfully. Maybe you do feel inauthentic, even though you try to tell yourself that it's not the case.

After you've finished this book and given yourself a little time to improve on these skills, come back and take the quiz again to see how things might have changed.

Body Scan

A body scan is a great way to go through your physical anatomy and become more connected with the body we have. Often, it can be hard to be confident because we are uncomfortable in the skin we've been given. You might struggle to love yourself or appreciate different aspects of your body. Getting comfortable with your body can make it easier to have confidence.

To do a body scan, you want to sit somewhere comfortable. Close your eyes and make sure that your body is completely stretched out. Focus on your breathing and count as you breathe in and out.

To begin the body scan, focus on the top of your head. Pay attention to the way that it feels and what its functions are. How does this make your head feel? How does your body feel overall in connection with your head?

Move down now to your forehead area. Think about what's underneath your forehead. Think about your skull. You can include gratitude practices in this by being thankful for each part of your body as you go down through the scan. Be grateful that you have a brain that can see, hear, and operate all the other functions necessary for you to exist.

Move to your eyes and your nose. Think of all the functions that these provide as well as your ears. Scan down to your jaw and your mouth. Feel as the air comes into your body and notice how all of this works together to keep you functioning in a healthy way.

Think about your neck and your shoulders and all the tension that might exist from the things that cause you so much stress. Breathe in and out as you feel some of this tension being released, especially in your chest area. Move down to your stomach and your waist and then to your legs all the way to your feet. Whenever you are feeling anxious or uncomfortable with your body, you can do this scan to get a little closer to yourself. It's a great way for you to be more connected to parts of yourself that you might feel completely disconnected from. Practice this when you're feeling stressed or anxious to help alleviate some of those feelings that keep you stuck in a negative headspace.

Find Your Anthem

Research shows that confidence can be increased with the use of certain songs (Hsu, Huang & Nordgren, 2014).

To boost your confidence, you should give yourself an anthem. Think of a song that makes you feel good about yourself. Don't pick one that you're just good at singing; think about one that really helps boost your confidence. It can be a specific artist or maybe just a classic tune. Think about movie soundtracks.

Pick anything, no matter how random, to become your anthem.

Sing it, learn the words and the melody, and get used to repeating this song. That way, this can become a boost of confidence that is needed. Whenever you are feeling stressed or disconnected from the world, you can give yourself the opportunity to be closer to feeling comfortable in your own skin and happy with who you are by playing the song.

Whenever you're sad or down, play the song and feel how good it makes you feel about yourself.

Take lyrics from the song and make art from it. Get a tattoo with the lyrics! Put a picture on your wall of some of the lyrics. Write some phrases on a Post-It note and put it on your mirror. Get a T-shirt with a slogan printed or the artist that you like on it.

Remind yourself of the powerful message of this song and sing it whenever you need to feel good. Have it downloaded on your phone so, whenever you are scared, you can listen to it and have it boost those necessary good emotions.

You should also curate different playlists for various moods. Don't just listen to the last thing that comes up on your shuffle. Try to come up with powerful and inspiring playlists that you can specifically pick to get into the right mindset when it's needed. Remember that there are different kinds of confidence as well. Maybe you have a playlist of high-energy, enthusiastic songs that you can play for working out and stay motivated. You can also come up with a playlist for more relaxing, confidence-boosting songs. These you might play before a date or maybe when you're getting ready for a party. They can relax you and make you feel good about yourself so you have that energy needed to function socially in that setting.

Pick a song that you enjoy that makes you happy. Don't let anybody make you feel guilty or embarrassed for the song you pick and remind

yourself you are amazing and you deserve to have
fun with music.

Chapter 3: Past Experiences That Shaped Our Personalities

It's important to remember that what you lived through has shaped your personality. The unique experiences that have opened your mind have also provided you with the basis for how you view the world now. This will ultimately be inclusive of the way you view yourself. Your self-esteem can be greatly affected by how you were raised to see yourself. Did your parents raise you to believe a certain truth about yourself? Were you led to believe various lies or truths about who you are as an individual? These are important aspects to reflect on to get a better understanding of who we are now.

The things that set us off and trigger us into feelings of self-doubt might be much different from what does the same to another individual. You'll have to look deep inside your past to recognize what you might have lived through that inspired the view you have of yourself now.

How the Past Relates to the Present

The experiences that we went through in the past will directly affect how we live now. To start, you can go back all the way to the biology and chemical makeup of the two people that created you.

Even if you have no idea who these individuals are, part of their genetics have been passed down to you. Some things we are just predisposed to have.

For example, if you were born with two very short parents, you might have a higher chance of being short now. That likely affected your life, especially if height altered what you wanted to cultivate in life. If you wanted to be a top basketball player, maybe that was challenging for you because of the genes that were passed down.

Before we were even able to open our eyes and look around this great earth, we were subjected to factors that were out of our control.

Moving on from there, you can take a further look at who was involved in raising you. This includes basic primary caregivers. For most people, that's a mother or father, stepparents, or perhaps grandparents, aunts, and uncles.

Aside from that, look at other people who played a role in your development. This includes older siblings. Maybe it's the neighbor and their children that you would always hang around with. It could also be a babysitter or a teacher.

These individuals influence how you operate within the world now. The past also relates to the present. For example, if you're 25 years old now and you lived through an abusive relationship at the age of 23, that's still going to affect you greatly now and for a while. Look at the stages of your life. You have "before," "in the beginning," and "what just happened."

These different areas of life are always going to play a role in how you interact with the world now.

How to Prevent Your Past from Impacting Your Present

Carrying the past into the future with you is a quick way to keep yourself trapped in a negative mindset. To overcome this, there are a few simple things you can begin to do.

This starts with recognizing what feelings you had during these moments.

You might have experienced times when you struggled because you felt like you didn't have any trust or support. These kinds of emotions can have negative effects on you because you want to be able to trust in the future. Unfortunately, the relationships we had growing up can teach us how to have relationships in the future. If you only know how to go about things in a negative, unhealthy way, of course, this kind of behavior is going to carry with you into adulthood.

One thing that you have to do to get over the past is to learn how to forgive those who might have harmed you.

Sometimes we hold on to resentment in our hearts because we have not yet understood where the other person came from. By gaining that perspective, you're able to find a new ability to work through those challenging feelings that they caused in the beginning. You can confront your childhood bully by going into their past and re-experiencing things from a new perspective.

If you are somebody who has always been a little bit more afraid of the outside world, then it's easy to continue to be scared as you go throughout your life.

You don't have to be the same person that you used to be. That is one essential part of building confidence. It's easy to stay stuck in the same mindset that you're always in. But you deserve to find a new ability to be confident.

Sometimes we have to let go of the past by removing ourselves from a place where we're afraid. If not, it's going to repeat itself.

If you are somebody who has experienced repeated traumatic things, it's easy to be afraid that they're going to happen again. This can easily destroy your confidence. If you've been cheated on once or even twice by an ex, you're going to have that fear that it may happen again. It can make you very insecure in your relationship. You might think they're constantly talking about, cheating on you, or losing interest easily.

These kinds of emotions are hard to deal with, but you can learn to overcome them. An essential part of moving past these processes is noticing and recognizing what trauma is.

Understanding Trauma

Trauma comes in many different forms. When we think of trauma, we might go straight to extremely challenging situations, such as warfare or terrible accidents. This is one of the first ways that we can process what it means to go through a traumatic experience. Somebody who lives with trauma has to recognize what it was that they went through in the first place. Not everyone realizes what they lived through was traumatic. Sometimes we are diminished in our feelings by others, or perhaps it is validation from within yourself that is lacking.

Someone who has experienced trauma will want to notice how their experiences relate to the way that they view the world now in order to begin overcoming it.

Trauma is something that many individuals go through.

It doesn't always look like obvious situations, such as accidents or extreme violence. Sometimes trauma can be neglect. It can be when we have basic needs deprived, such as food or water.

It might simply be witnessing trauma or noticing that you are surrounded by traumatic experiences. In some situations, even reading different news articles could be considered traumatic. What you are exposed to online can greatly affect what you are afraid of in the real world.

All of this is important to recognize so you can begin to overcome your trauma.

If you went through a horrific experience, such as sexual assault, domestic violence, seeing dead bodies, or other physical threats, you're never going to "just get over it." It's not something that you forget about and move on from. However, you can begin to build the confidence to confront these triggers as they come to you.

Triggers are another important part of understanding how to build your confidence. Despite the past experiences that you lived through, whatever challenging emotions or terrible scenarios in the past that you were submerged in, you can move on from those now.

You can begin to create a new life that isn't surrounded and engulfed with horrific trauma.

Instead, you can begin to move past any violence that you've been sentenced to. It's not easy, but when you begin to identify those triggers, you will be able to move on.

Identifying Triggers

When we talk about triggers, this refers to any kind of emotion that is brought up by a specific situation you went through. Not every kind of trauma is going to have a clear trigger. For example, think of a soldier who fought in a war. A trigger for them could be anything related to guns if they lived through a traumatic experience with this kind of weapon. This is a symbol that the brain associated with the pain it felt previously.

This person with that trigger might have a run-in with a gun, from seeing one on a police officer to just catching an image of one in a movie trailer. This could be enough to trigger them back into the mindset when they were in the middle of a war. It will click in their brain that they're living through that experience again, and their mind kind of goes into autopilot. The brain sees that trigger and thinks that it's going to be going through that trauma. All of a sudden, it will prepare the mind to put up with those issues, which can often take us back to the mental state we were in when we first experienced that trauma.

The trigger isn't always specific to that situation but, instead, something that induces those same feelings. If a soldier hears a car backfire that can sound like a gunshot and even though it has no relation to guns, it could still trigger that soldier back to the mindset they were in when they were fighting in the war. This could elicit any type of fight-or-flight response, such as lashing out at others or even attacking someone they perceived as a threat.

Triggers can also be random for some people. We don't always have control over when something is triggering. You might think you can go up a flight of stairs, but perhaps the steepness is enough to trigger you back to a time when you were afraid of heights.

Something as simple as a flash in memory could pull somebody back into that panic state and cause an attack. Any feelings that are evoked that remind an individual of the trauma they've been through can keep them in that same mindset. These feelings include the following:

- exclusion
- powerlessness
- loneliness
- neglect
- manipulation
- frustration
- entrapment

Any time you feel unsafe or unprepared, identifying these triggers makes it easier to remind yourself that you are safe and protected.

Anti-Anxiety Exercises

These exercises are specifically designed to help you get through your past experiences. You won't want to forget them, but it is important to move on from the feelings they've left you with.

Though our traumas are individual, we have all earned a similar understanding of the world after experiencing moments of low self-esteem. It's not easy to dislike who you are and lack the confidence to be a more assertive person. We know what it means to be fearful of another person, and we can easily recognize when someone is feeling scared or worried, so that has helped us to develop empathy. These activities are going to help keep you mindful and be in the moment to see reality. You'll be able to find a clear and present perspective on what's actually occurring when you pay attention to what's around you.

Reflecting is an important part of the process of understanding the past experiences that have shaped our personalities. The more you emphasize finding a greater truth to this, the easier it will be for you to overcome the negative feelings you have about yourself.

Mindfulness

Mindfulness is one of the best activities you can use to help alleviate stressful and anxious feelings. Mindfulness involves first simply becoming aware of your surroundings. This will include paying attention to things that you are with at this moment. There are a few methods of mindfulness that can be very helpful for wherever you are. Whether you are in the comfort of your own home and stressed out or sitting in the bathroom at work before making a huge presentation, mindfulness can take you where your mind needs to be.

The first method of mindfulness is to pick a single color. Look around the room and identify everything that is the same color as this. Stick to something basic at first. This could be green. You notice the green plants in the window. The video game controller is green. The lighter on the table is green. The book on the bookshelf is green. The candle is green. The candy wrapper is green.

After doing this, you'll notice that your mind is no longer stuck on the things that were making you anxious, and instead, you are present right in this moment. You can get more specific and take the rules further. Pick out anything that's wood. What's plastic? What might be shiny, matte, soft, or rough? Work through these over and over again until your mind is blank and you're no longer running with those ruminations.

The second act of mindfulness is what many refer to as their five senses. The rules are as follows:

1. Identify five things you can see.
2. Identify four things you can touch.
3. Identify three things you can hear.
4. Identify two things you can smell.
5. Identify one thing you can taste.

Now you don't actually have to taste or smell anything. The things you identify don't even have to be common-odor objects. They don't have to be edible. You are just identifying these things. If you're at home, this is probably easy. Here are some examples:

1. "I can see the couch, dining room table, TV, rug, and cat."
2. "I can touch the blanket, pillow, hardwood floor, and computer."
3. "I can hear the dogs barking outside, the hand of the clock ticking, and the heater running."
4. "I can smell the air freshener and brewed coffee."
5. "I can taste the glass of water."

This is a very basic method and helps to activate your mind, so you are focused on what is right in front of you.

Sometimes these things aren't easy to identify. Remember, you can get a little creative with it! Let's say you're in the doctor's office and it's a pretty boring waiting room. You're extremely nervous because you hate the doctors. You're thinking of all the terrible things they might diagnose you with, and having to step on the scale and get weighed is also causing you to panic. Try the "five senses" activity! It's a lot harder to find things to smell or taste, but not impossible:

1. "I see the clerk, coffee table, magazine rack, plastic plant, and box of tissues."
2. "I can touch my purse, my jeans, the metal armchair, and the brochure on insurance."
3. "I can hear the doctor laughing in the other room, the traffic outside, and the sound of the clerk typing."
4. "I can smell the stale carpet that has probably been in the office for decades, and I can smell my own perfume."
5. "I can taste the hand sanitizer sitting on the clerk's desk."

It's not about actually doing these things but simply identifying what it would be like to live through those senses. You can take mindfulness even further and combine these activities! For example, identify one red thing you can see or identify one blue thing you can hear.

These are harder, but they can help you focus when you are running over pointless scary thoughts in your mind.

Acceptance and Commitment Therapy

Acceptance and commitment therapy (ACT) is a form of therapy used for confronting reactions to various stressors. The idea behind ACT is to confront those negative inner emotions that cause the individual to struggle. These feelings include things like guilt, regret, stress, panic, and worry over things that are usually out of the individual's control. ACT strives to help individuals recognize that their thoughts aren't to be ignored and we can't just hope they'll go away. Instead, this kind of therapy can be used to confront negative emotions to learn how to embrace them rather than ignoring them.

Sometimes you simply have to accept that you are going to have negative emotions. These are either going to help you learn something, or they are just moments that you have to let pass.

To use some ACT techniques, you have to start reflecting on the language that you're using with yourself. With an ACT therapist, they will usually go over this with you and identify that, but on your own, you can still use some of these methods to help alleviate constant negative emotions.

By suppressing certain feelings, you might end up causing even more panic or worry because you're not confronting the issue at hand.

The steps for acceptance therapy are as follows:

1. Notice the way that you feel. Pay attention to your reactions to an issue that's been presented to you.
2. Decide whether this is a situation that can be changed or not. Gauge how much power or control you have over the situation.
3. If the situation can be changed, change it.
4. If the situation cannot be changed, change your emotion.
5. If your emotions and situation cannot be changed, embrace this feeling and reflect on how it is affecting your life.

6. Make a commitment to yourself to try to change these emotions actively and prevent them from happening in the future.

ACT is all about recognizing negative patterns or behaviors and promising yourself that you are not going to let this happen again. You are accepting that you have certain emotions and then committing yourself to overcoming these in the best way possible.

Interoceptive Exposure

The point of interoceptive exposure is to remind you that you are safe and protected even in times when you might feel that's not the case. There are different physical symptoms that panic and worry can cause. If you have chronic anxiety, you've likely experienced these discomforts:

- Fast breathing
- Racing heartbeat
- Muscle strain
- Sweating

If you're anxious, then you're already worried and freaking out. Then imagine that you are anxious, and you start breathing heavily. Those kinds of physical symptoms can also alter your levels of anxiety. This could end up in you becoming more anxious just because you're already anxious!

Interoceptive exposure takes some of these symptoms and forces you to live through them. You go into prepared and ready to remind your brain that you are safe and protected. You will let your body know that whatever it is experiencing at this moment is not bad and will not cause harm.

The first interoceptive exposure activity is to breathe fast. To do this, over-breathe as if you just ran a mile or more. Pretend as though you just came up ten flights of stairs. Breathe rapidly for no longer than a minute.

Afterward, reflect on how you feel. What is it that kept you feeling anxious? What was the hardest part? You can try these other breathing-restrictive exercises:

- Breathing through a straw with your nose plugged
- Gently covering your mouth and nose with your hand to restrict some of your breathing
- Holding your breath for no more than 30-second intervals

Never do this for longer than a minute at the most (besides holding your breath, never go longer than what you physically can). The point is to not make you sick or dizzy. You are simply showing your body that going through these motions does not mean you are going to die. Instead, you are building your skills and training yourself to power through as needed.

Another activity you can do is to tense your body. For 20 seconds at the most, try to tense every single muscle in your body. Afterward, notice how it makes you feel.

What was the hardest part of this? What made it difficult for you to push through at times? Reflect this in your journal if you have one, or at least take a moment to reflect on your thoughts. These aren't things to do daily, but repeating them a few times can help you get used to these physical sensations to make it easier to work through a panic attack later on.

Chapter 4: Roots of Low Self-Esteem

Our self-esteem didn't just randomly appear. When you consider why you might struggle with certain aspects of life, it can be easily followed along a path back to where your life really began. What most don't realize is that the things they were subjected to overtime have played into how they interact with the world now. You were raised to view the world in a certain way, and that has certainly become a part of how you view what is "normal."

Some people were taught that they should be ashamed of their behaviors or that any sense of pride is a bad quality. Others were taught to constantly hold their head high, but maybe to a fault. To fully grasp why you experience the self-esteem you do now, it's important to start by turning the clock back and reflecting on past experiences.

Self-Image Issues

Any issue that you might have dealing with your self-esteem usually has a root back in your history. You can go back to this time and see how it might have affected the way you view yourself now. There are a few factors that go into having self-esteem issues. One factor is having parents who were hard on you when you were growing up and who were often disapproving.

Even if you were a successful child who constantly got good grades, you might have struggled to get any form of approval out of them. This can lead to you having issues with overcoming feelings of self-doubt now. They might have actively instilled negative thoughts in you. They might have told you that you're not good enough or that they were never proud of you. Those feelings can keep us lacking self-esteem because it goes all the way back to our roots. From the moment that we were able to begin to comprehend what it meant to feel good about ourselves, we might have also been taught to question our own abilities.

If you were neglected as a child, this could often affect your self-esteem. Now, you might be constantly unsure of yourself, wondering if you have any value based on what you're able to offer others.

If you were bullied a lot as a child, this would have a deep negative impact on you now. It can cause you to feel like you are the things your bullies told you that you were.

It can keep you feeling constantly negative about yourself, always questioning your worth.

You might struggle with self-esteem as an adult because, as a child, you were never responsible for yourself. This could be the case for individuals who have parents who are overbearing or overprotective. When a parent is in control, it can mean their child never had to take action to get something done. This might have been in someone else's hands. It could have been that there were different individuals who were able to help give you the answers you needed rather than discovering them on your own. Perhaps you never had to think for yourself or solve your own problems because somebody else was doing that for you.

It might have sounded like a luxury for some individuals, but this can also have us lacking self-esteem now. Those who have gone through having overbearing parents don't have to question themselves and look at their weaknesses, wondering if they're making the right decision.

As we discussed in the previous chapter, anything dealing with trauma could have you lacking self-esteem now. How people perceived you or treated you in the past could affect your current perspective.

Understanding Perspective

Your perspective is how you absorb the world around you. It's also how you believe you are perceived in other people. Your perspective includes your ability to evaluate a situation. Do you perceive things as being good or bad? Two people can have opposite perceptions of the same situation. It's all about past circumstances and present positions that will alter how we perceive the world.

How were you treated throughout your life? This can also change your perspective. If you have many different adversities you've lived through, that gives you a much different perspective than somebody who's had more privileges.

It's important to understand the perception that you didn't have control over that has caused you to view yourself in a certain way now.

If you lived through much trauma and terrible situations, it's easy to have a negative perspective now. You might view the world as a scary and dangerous place. You can constantly be stressed about things that other people don't even think twice about.

It's not easy to deal with these kinds of struggles, but it is very normal because that's how we judge the world. You base things on how you were taught. You base things on what you grew to believe. If you were taught to judge people very harshly by the way they look, that changes the perception that you have of yourself now. Look at how you might perceive the situation that somebody else doesn't. In the same way, maybe you know somebody who doesn't seem to care at all about keeping their house clean, or maybe they never have trimmed nails or brushed hair. Perhaps somebody never has any money or nice things. Maybe some of this you care about and some you don't. All these opinions on what is important make up our perception. It changes how we view the world around us and what we believe is important in life. Our perceptions can lead us into different convictions, and if we're not careful, these can control our lives. They can become our virtues and our constant beliefs that shaped not only how we behave in the world but also how we're treated by other people. If you practice enough, you can turn these convictions into feelings and have them be things that aid you in creating a healthier level of confidence.

Turning Convictions Into Feelings

First, identify what convictions you carry about yourself. Do you believe that nobody likes you? Do you perceive that you're often ignored? Perhaps you have the impression that other people do not care about your opinion. All of this can affect your convictions. You can set yourself up for negative prophecies for how you go about a situation. Perhaps you always self-sabotage your relationships. Maybe you continue to fall back into unhealthy patterns that you are actively trying to break. You might struggle to maintain a consistent period of employment.

You might have certain rules or commandments you have for yourself. Maybe you're not allowed to enjoy certain things and you often punish or torture yourself based on minor behavior. For example, maybe you are constantly at the gym. If you indulge in a fast-food meal once a week, you might torture yourself by going extra hard at the gym to the point that you strain your muscles.

Oppositely, you might punish yourself by then binge-eating to the point that you're sick to your stomach because you're disappointed and already broke your diet.

Sometimes these convictions can feel normal. They happen so frequently we don't even recognize we are the ones in charge of them.

Begin to recognize these convictions and notice how they are simply feelings. You do not have to torture yourself. There is no sort of enforcement over your own body. It is you who decides how you feel and how you interact with the world.

Use that self-doubt and turn it into a way to reflect actively on what you need to improve on. Maybe you do fall back into the same habits over and over again. That consistency can be beneficial in other ways. If you're good at falling into habits, make them healthy habits. If it's easy for you to be dependent on certain rituals, make them ones that aid in your life, and improve things for the better.

These convictions should be motivations, not things that restrict you that you have to follow so staunchly.

There are a few wrong intellectual beliefs you might have that can keep you trapped in a fixed mindset. A fixed mindset is when you don't allow yourself to fully embrace all of the great knowledge there is to absorb in the world.

A fixed mindset is when you don't allow yourself to explore everything around you. It's a way that your brain might be trapped in the same place. It's easy to fall into negative habits and not grow or become a better individual when you have a fixed mindset.

The Wrong Intellectual Beliefs

These forms of beliefs about ourselves that we follow can turn into how we behave within the world. For example, one "wrong" intellectual belief that you should let go of is the idea that you are already as smart as you can be. Some people believe that they truly know everything. Even if they're not familiar with the subject, they might relate it to one that they do know. Perhaps if somebody shares information, they come back by saying, "Oh yeah, I already knew that."

These kinds of mindsets prevent that individual from learning things in a new and abstract way. They might take more information in, but it's only on their own terms, so it is going to be biased to their perspective only.

Nobody knows everything. In fact, the more somebody knows, the more they realize they have an entire universe of knowledge left to absorb. There is never too much information in the world.

This leads to another false belief that too many people adopt. You should not reject constructive criticism from somebody who's trying to share what they believe you might need to improve on. Take that in.

Embrace what their words are trying to tell you to become a better individual. These don't have to be things that destroy your self-esteem and instead can become the exact things that build you into a more confident person. Don't be threatened by the success of the people around you.

Don't feel like you are in competition with them. Give yourself the ability to be your own biggest competitor. Actively choose to be better than the individual that you were yesterday.

Constantly challenge your beliefs about yourself. If you look in the mirror and you think to yourself, "I'm ugly," "I'm worthless," or "I have nothing to offer," question where that thought came from. Is that true?

What facts do you have to prove the legitimacy? Did somebody else tell you this? Maybe you look in the mirror and call yourself a specific name that a bully used to refer to you as. Go back in time and reflect on that bullying. Why do you think they stated that to you?

As an adult, we can look at children now and recognize that those who bullied us in the past were likely experiencing similar treatment in a home setting.

Once you begin to unravel these thoughts, you dive deep into the root of your self-esteem and how to improve and enhance what are seemingly negative qualities.

Reflection Exercises

When you learn how to reflect on yourself and your past, it becomes easier to avoid low self-esteem. Looking for the root of where these feelings derived is one of the easiest ways to get over them.

It's not easy to get over your past. It won't occur overnight, and it will take time to break down the ideas that you have built around yourself. Acknowledgment is the first step, and you've already completed this part! Now it is time to look for ways to dive even further into the root of your self-esteem issues. You are powerful enough to overcome these doubtful and stressed-out feelings, so remember that with enough effort and dedication, you can begin to rework the way your brain operates. Take small steps to get there. You likely built ideas that validate your low self-esteem for a very long time, so be kind to yourself in this process and know that it's not going to happen so quickly.

Memory Maps

There are likely a lot of things in your brain that you have forgotten about. The thing about our brains is that it has unlimited storage. There's really never a maximum for what you can remember or know.

As you go throughout your journey of building confidence, there are going to be a lot of self-reflection exercises, as you've already seen in this book alone.

A memory map can be a great way to help bring things back up. This reflection exercise gives you the ability to look deep into your past to get a better understanding of the things you might have gone through that led to where you are today.

To use a memory map, begin by coming up with a specific scenario that you want to recall. Maybe you're trying to think back to your childhood. Perhaps there are moments in school or with other clubs or activities that you wish you could recall. Get a piece of paper and a writing tool. Draw the best map from memory that you can.

This should be of the physical location that you were in during the moment you are trying to remember.

If you want to recall perhaps getting bullied in elementary school, draw your elementary school from memory in a blueprint-style map. You can use a bird's-eye perspective. Travel through this map and see what memories you can bring up. You can also look at pictures, and you can even start to make more detailed and descriptive maps to dive further into your memory.

Finish the Movie

Sometimes we have a terrifying script in our mind of what the future is going to look like. By giving yourself the chance to work through this first on your own, you can discover that the worst-case scenario is never as bad as you think it's going to be.

For this activity, you want to take a situation that you are afraid of having and let it all play out until the end. Even if the next things that happen aren't what you like, continue going through with the ideas of what you're expecting to happen.

This activity requires you to continue playing out the moments that you might cut off.

It's a visualization exercise that will give you the opportunity to see the future in a few different ways.

Let's say that you are really stressed out because you're texting a girl that you hope to date and she's not responding. The two of you went on a date together, and it seems like she's just never around her phone when you text her.

You want to hang out again, but you never really get that response from her. This leads to intense anxious thoughts. One thing that can help you through is to play the movie until the end.

Often, people will play the movie just until the middle, and they'll go over a million different scenes. They never get to the end where they realize their worries aren't as big as they thought.

You think about how she's not texting you back because she's with other guys. She doesn't like you, so she's not responding. She's making fun of you to all her friends, which is why she's not near her phone. None of these are true, and you get stuck playing the same middle scene over and over.

You want to completely finish that out. Go to the end of your movie.

What happens in the perfect movie? You might date her, fall in love, get married, have children live a happy life together, and die of old age in bed next to one another. That's a wonderful movie.

That will only happen if she likes you back and responds.

Rather than thinking about yourself, think about her. Maybe she doesn't want that same movie. Maybe she's not the girl for you to complete that movie. Maybe you go on the second date and realize you're repulsed by her. You're only in the beginning, yet you're letting that completely ruin your emotions. Wait until the end!

The focus is instead on the singular instance that can become the negative situation that ruins your week.

Become Your Own Superhero

Mixed martial arts fighters have been known to adopt an alter-ego to help them alternate between various levels of confidence.

As a little kid, you might have had somebody that you looked up to who made you feel protected. Maybe Spider-Man was always there to help you fight off anything that you needed. Perhaps you enjoyed more literal figures, such as powerful detectives in criminal justice shows or animal researchers on your favorite nature documentary.

Whoever your heroes were as a child might still be there now, or they might have faded. Now what you need is to become your own superhero. To begin, pick out what your superpower might be. If you don't have weird mystical powers like becoming invisible (like most of us), then you can pick out other things like helping other people, cooking, drawing, figuring out problems, and so on.

Any of these situations could be your superpower and something that helps you become the best version of yourself. Create a persona in your mind of somebody who is unstoppable. Envision that movie situation we just discussed and picture how you would be able to fight things off. If you believe in yourself and know that, at the end of the day, you will be the hero coming out safe, it makes you feel more protected and calmer, increasing your confidence.

Chapter 5: Overcome Perfectionism

Perfectionism is a big reason we struggle with self-esteem.

Always wanting to be flawless and having anxiety over failure and mistakes can keep us constantly panicked. If you find one minor flaw in yourself, it can become shockingly easy to let this be the reason why you view yourself as a failure. Repeatedly believing you are not a successful individual can take a huge toll on how you view yourself. Alternating perspectives can confuse us as well. Other people who don't have perfectionist tendencies might see you and tell you how great or valuable you are. However, you don't see that yourself, so it could be challenging to trust what others are saying. Are they lying to you? Are they just trying to win you over or manipulate you with their kind words? This kind of confusion can keep us afraid of the outside world, always questioning who might be on our side and who might be out to get us.

Signs of Perfectionism

Perfectionism is one pattern of thinking that can keep us in a place of low self-esteem. Perfectionists aren't people who just do things "perfectly." It's not somebody who is good at everything or always gets stuff done necessarily. That could be the case, but it doesn't always equate to each other. A perfectionist is all about the way a person views themselves. They frequently believe that they are either good or bad and nothing in between. This is a type of all-or-nothing thinking. It can make the perfectionist in them very judgmental and critical of themselves. It's easy to have a one-sided perspective when one has perfectionist qualities.

A perfectionist will be extremely critical. They'll have great attention to detail, and they'll notice minor imperfections. The thing about perfectionists is they will let these minor things drive them to a place of high anxiety. If they look in the mirror and have flawless makeup but notice one smudge on their lipstick, they'll end up feeling very self-conscious, and that will ruin the idea that they are beautiful. They might have had a seven-day vacation, and all six days were great until the last day when they missed their flight.

All of a sudden, that ruins the vacation and leaves them feeling as though they are unsuccessful. Perfectionists will also struggle because they believe they have to meet extreme, unrealistic standards that nobody necessarily placed on them. Often, these ideas and pressures can develop from within the individual on their own time through years of changing perspectives.

All-or-Nothing Thought Patterns

Let's look a little bit further now what all-or-nothing thinking is. All-or-nothing thinking is a cognitive distortion that we discussed earlier. It's especially challenging for people who are perfectionists.

You might believe you are either a failure or a success. The qualifications that make you successful are much stricter than what you might use to label yourself as a failure. If you get three 10/10 ratings on quizzes, you might think this is normal or standard. Then the 9/10 will be your downfall and make you feel as though you're a total failure just because of that 1 point off out of 40 possible points.

The thing about all-or-nothing thinkers is that they love to label. They will label themselves as good or bad based on one circumstance, rather than looking at the overall picture.

To overcome all-or-nothing thinking, remember that you are not one singular instance. If you are any sort of performer, athlete, or somebody else who has instances where they might be judged, don't let one bad time make you feel as though you are unsuccessful every other time.

As a perfectionist with an all-or-nothing-thinking type of habits, remember to find the balance. You don't always have to be blindly positive. It's healthy to reflect on your negative qualities. Don't ruminate on them. If that's the only thing that you hang on to, it will leave you feeling very hopeless and lost. Notice when you might have made a mistake or when there are things you can improve on, but remind yourself not to obsess over these things.

Always question facts, as well as your thoughts, and remember that you are better than the worst things you might believe about yourself.

Procrastination

Sometimes we procrastinate because of the fear over failure. We might be so overwhelmed by goals that we keep pushing these things off. Too much procrastination will eventually lead to unrealistic standards.

Procrastination is very common for perfectionists. You might think that a perfectionist would be very good at having a schedule and sticking to it. Unfortunately, it can be quite the opposite. A perfectionist can be obsessive about getting everything right to the point that they continue to push things further and further back.

Sometimes they simply can't get a task done unless they do it absolutely perfectly. This is very toxic to these types of thinkers because they will always struggle to see reality.

A procrastinator does so because they don't want to have to face potential failure.

Sometimes putting something off also means putting devastation off. A procrastinator procrastinates because they will have to feel that rejection if things don't go as perfectly as they've predicted.

They won't have to feel negative about themselves in any way if they don't do the task at all.

Sometimes perfectionists will wait for the perfect moment to get something done. You might want to wait until after your vacation to start your diet. You may as well enjoy the trip, right? Then you want to diet before the next vacation, but then that comes and passes, so you wait until afterward again.

A perfectionist might constantly be seeking out that perfect moment in an attempt to try to prolong and procrastinate.

Maybe you need to get a report done for work, but the dishes need to be done. You do the dishes, and then you want to finish painting the walls of the bathroom. Then you have to go and pull weeds from the garden. It's easy to continue to find methods to procrastinate, especially for perfectionists who feel as though they're being productive.

While you might need to do all those little tasks, it can also detract from what needs to be done.

Causes for Perfectionism

Most importantly, there are many causes for perfectionism that can help you better understand why you have these feelings and urges. Perfectionism is often a way to handle trauma, especially for something that we experienced as children. Perfectionism provides us with an instant release of pain.

If you focus on all the little minor details of one aspect of life, you can easily ignore another. Perfectionism occurs because, rather than dealing with negative emotions and confronting the challenging traumas you live through, you cling yourself onto obsessive details, such as getting good grades or having the perfect look.

Think of somebody who might have been abused as a child, so now they seek out constant plastic surgery. They might be on the hunt for the perfect face even though the one they started with was fine. They might have been bullied, so they're constantly seeking out better situations they can do to help them overcome those feelings.

Perfectionism is something that can be overcome. It's not easy, it's not quick, and it's not painless. However, with the right aspects and willingness to live through some of these things, you can overcome perfectionism in the end.

Emotional Consequences of Past Expectations

Often, perfectionism comes because of the pressures we might have felt as a child.

There are emotional consequences of perfectionism. What you should understand is that regret and the remorse over not using your time efficiently can take a toll on you. This can lead to having high expectations for goals that you set in the future. Maybe you look in the past and think to yourself, "How could I have not completed that goal over this period of time?"

When you look back over five years of your life that you might have wanted to lose weight, it's easy to think, "How could I have not lost the weight?"

Now you set extreme goals for yourself trying to make up for the lost time. This can destroy our confidence. You set these extreme goals, you don't make them, and then it leaves you feeling upset. When you aren't successful, that takes a toll on your ability to have high self-esteem because you eventually won't believe in yourself when you're constantly letting yourself down from not achieving these insanely high goals.

Begin to allow yourself to overcome your past experiences. Forgive that regret and remorse you have, and realize you weren't in control of every situation that you lived through.

Perfectionist-Breaking Exercises

If you are a perfectionist, then you already have a way that you operate with the world around you. These might include routines or schedules that you have to participate in, or else it might cause panic. These aren't normal routines, like brushing your teeth before bed or getting up and working out. They are routines that might go unnoticed, like asking for an extension, not fulfilling that, getting angry at yourself, working last minute, and then repeating the cycle for the next project. By including these kinds of mental exercises in your life, you're enabling yourself to overcome these bad habits and replace them with new, healthier ones.

ABC Functional Analysis

An ABC analysis is perfect for those who want to try out different methods of cognitive behavioral therapy (CBT). There are three steps involved in conducting an ABC analysis. It stands for the following:

- Behavior
- Antecedents
- Consequences

To begin, you want to first identify your behavior. Is this destructive, disruptive, or dangerous? Do you often avoid certain situations because of the emotions it might bring up? Are you always looking for a way to avoid your problems? Perhaps you are struggling with an addiction of some sort.

To do this analysis, you can write in your journal, or simply mentally reflect as we take you through the process.

Pick out whatever problematic behavior you have. You can create a chart so that you do this with multiple issues rather than just one at a time. It's fine to go at your own pace, however, and don't overwhelm yourself by doing it all at once!

The antecedents are any events that you live through before this behavior that might have led to the current situation. Did you experience childhood trauma or abuse? Were you taught this behavior throughout your life? Was it something more recent you went through that is causing the issues?

The third column would then be "consequences," if you are making a chart. This is simply the third step if you're doing it mentally only.

Consequences are everything that you might have lived through that was a result of this kind of behavior. What have you experienced that led you to be the individual you are now? What did you live through that was a result of something bad you did first?

You can try this activity every time you have a problem so that you can do a proper analysis of what it caused and affected. Below, we have a chart to give you an idea of how you can begin to use an ABC analysis to understand your biggest issues.

Antecedents	Behavior	Consequences
"My parents were very hard on me and often told me I wasn't good	"I can't stand to look in the mirror at myself." "I rarely talk to	"I isolate myself and have very few friends." "I don't go out of my way to try

enough." "I was made fun of for the way that I looked." "I was an outcast in school because of my religion."	other people because I don't like the things I say."	new things." "I am struggling to find a job because I don't have the confidence to make it through an interview."

When you lay out your issues analytically, it's much easier to break them apart and find the areas that you can begin to improve on. Clearly, the issue here would be parental figures, appearance perspective, and social outcast. The issue might not be the way someone looks but how they were taught to view themselves. It's only when doing an analytic breakdown of these things can you begin to discover what the root of the problem might be.

The Four Ps of Perfectionism

To break down why you have perfectionist tendencies, you can evaluate four different *P* factors:

- Predisposing
- Precipitating
- Perpetuating
- Protective

When struggling with perfection, you can break these areas of a problem down to help you unravel back to the roots, making it easier to overcome these issues.

This is important for your confidence levels because it is often our perfectionist pressures that make us feel as though we don't have the ability to have control over our emotions.

To start by doing the four *P*s, pick out a problem.

This can be very specific, like "I never finish a project on time because I am always stressed about what will happen, and I push it off until the last minute to avoid feelings of failure."

It could also be general, such as "I am a perfectionist."

The first step of the four *Ps* is to look at predisposing factors. What things were out of your control, and what natural or genetic characteristics have affected this situation? Predisposing factors include the following things:

- Age
- Life events
- Trauma
- Childhood experiences
- Genetics
- Environment

These are all things that put you at risk for developing perfectionist qualities. Intense parents that put a lot of pressure on you is a predisposing factor that was out of your control. Getting sent to a highly strict and competitive school was also something you had little power over. Your race or religion might be something that makes you a minority, depending on the area, putting you at risk for various adversities that you have no control over.

The second *P* is about looking at specific situations that have triggered this issue. These are things that you might have more control over, but they are also inclusive of instances of trauma. You are going to identify the things that actually relate to the situation. If you are struggling because of the first problem we identified with procrastinating problems, this evaluation might include the time that you failed a project, and it affected your self-esteem to this day. It might have been a time that you were grounded for getting bad grades, leading to you getting grounded and maybe missing out on something exciting like homecoming or prom.

The third *P* is all about looking at what you currently do that keeps fueling this issue. Do you sit in bed when you work on your projects? It's likely easy to turn on the TV or scroll your phone if you're wrapped up under the blankets while trying to finish an assignment. Maybe you are purposely scheduling other things first to keep pushing this off. Look at what your current behaviors are that are negatively impacting your ability to get over these types of issues.

The final *P* is to look at the positive aspects of your life that can help you overcome this related stress. For example, having access to a university library means that you have a safe space to go to study without getting distracted. Having current good grades means that you have a reminder and validation that you are capable of achieving success and you shouldn't be so stressed about your performance.

Create a chart and fill out these four *P*s whenever you identify a perfectionist-related problem.

Thought Experiments

To break down perfectionism, you can start to track your behavior based on the thoughts that

you're having as if you are your own brain's
scientist.

Conducting a thought experiment helps to take
you to the next level. Often, we cut our thoughts
off because they can be scary if we aren't careful!
You might not want to picture the worst-case
scenario, or perhaps you start to grow concerned
over the images of something terrible happening.

Your thoughts alone could traumatize you if
you're not careful. That doesn't mean that we
should avoid playing through our thoughts.

To conduct thought experiments, get creative and
start to truly imagine what could potentially
happen. At any time, we are subjected to random
chance, but at such a small level that this is not
what you should be clinging to during these
thought experiments.

The point of a thought experiment is to help you
solve issues that aren't ones that normally make
you comfortable. Step outside of an area where
you feel emotionally secure and play with those

thoughts and feelings that might stretch beyond your comfort zone. During these thought experiments, you might discover that sometimes you will have to simply embrace the unknown.

You might be sitting there wondering, "Well, how is this different from rumination? I have thought experiments all the time when I'm driving or zoning out watching TV as I think about the things that stress me out."

That's the thing — those aren't thought experiments but directionless ruminations.

Think of your brain like a faucet. In life, you want to simply fill up a glass of water. The more your cup is filled, the more success in life, but that all depends on filling the cup with the stream of water that is your brain.

When you ruminate, it's like turning the faucet on full force but there is a leak, causing it to explode everywhere. You might be able to fill up some of the glass, but you're going to make a mess along the way.

Look for that steady stream.

Any scientific experiment has a similar process behind it that allows you to explore a greater truth. Take your mind through this same thought process to get a deeper idea of what your stresses, worries, and anxieties are. These are the steps:

1. *Observe:* What do you notice about your behavior or confidence?
2. *Question:* What question can you ask yourself about this that can help you overcome your worries? (For example, "Why am I so afraid to go to this job interview?")
3. *Research:* Find facts that can help you prove some of the thoughts you might have. (For example, "I have gotten plenty of jobs in the past, but I have also struggled in my interviews recently.")
4. *Hypothesize:* Come up with what you think the issue might be. (For example, "I'm afraid of the interview because of my past experiences.")

5. *Experiment:* Go through different situations in your mind. (For example, "Picture yourself at the job interview. Think of the best- and worst-case scenarios.")

6. *Test your hypothesis:* Do you feel as though this was a true statement? (For example, "Going back into my history reminds me that I have been made to have very little confidence, which affects my professional performance.")

7. *Draw conclusions:* What can you do now to help fix the hypothesis? (For example, "I can start to work through my past issues to help my future self get a job.")

Go through these steps with different issues to really break down what the core of your confidence problems might be.

A Short message from the Author:

Hey, are you enjoying the book? I'd love to hear your thoughts!

Many readers do not know how hard reviews are to come by, and how much they help an author.

I would be incredibly grateful if you could take just 60 seconds to write a brief review on Amazon, even if it's just a few sentences!

>> Scan the Barcode with your phone camera to leave a quick review;

Thank you for taking the time to share your thoughts!

Your review will genuinely make a difference for me and help gain exposure for my work.

Chapter 6: The Dangers of Imposter Syndrome

Imposter syndrome is something that gets talked about a little less than perfectionism, but it's likely something that you suffer with if you constantly struggle with self-doubt.

Even when we are successful, we can still feel as though we are failures. The feelings you have inside yourself have nothing to do with what your current situation is.

OK, well, not "nothing to do." They can influence how you feel, but they shouldn't! Regardless of where you are in life, you have to learn how to love and trust yourself. If you can't do this, it will end up hurting you in the long run. If you can't be satisfied with who you are and where you're at in life now, then how can you expect to be in any other situation.

Regardless of whether you have a lot of successes or failures under your belt, you could still struggle with debilitating self-doubt that keeps you from achieving your dreams.

What Is Imposter Syndrome?

Imposter syndrome is the idea that one is still not good enough even though there is clear and real proof that this is not the case. A person who is a perfectionist, consistently putting pressure on themselves and struggling with their self-image, might have imposter syndrome.

Those who feel inadequate even though they've been able to show high success levels often struggle with overwhelming and debilitating self-doubt (Corkindale, 2008).

Those who struggle deeply with confidence might also suffer from what is referred to as imposter syndrome. This is any type of feeling where you never feel good enough, even though you do have proof of success. Sometimes it's easy to feel inadequate because of our circumstances. Maybe you're single, unemployed, don't have a great house, or very unhappy with your level of attractiveness. These things are still relative, but they might be factors that keep us in a place of low self-esteem. Those who have imposter syndrome often have success in all these areas, yet they still feel deep low self-esteem. It's not that one person should have more self-esteem than another (as we should all strive to have the same amount in a way), but all people should recognize their accomplishments in a way that helps them feel better about themselves.

Those who suffer from imposter syndrome often feel like they cannot fail, or else it'll be the end of the world.

The idea of getting a bad grade on a test or getting in trouble at work can be debilitating. In fact, it is often this kind of fear that might be the reason they don't succeed in the end.

Imposters feel just as that — an imposter. They feel like they're fake. They feel like they don't fit in where they belong. They might wake up every day, not knowing who they are.

This kind of feeling can be because of all the pressure we've experienced throughout our lives. We often absorb the ideas, wants, and desires of other people, so after a certain point, it becomes difficult to know what we actually want versus what others have convinced us that we want. Imposters often become afraid that they'll be found out. They worry other people are going to notice that they have these flaws or that they might be deceptive because of their weaknesses in certain areas. Imposters often feel like they don't deserve the worth that they have. They fear other people see right through them and think they only are where they're at because of luck.

Imposter syndrome can make an individual feel like they're gambling with their success.

They don't recognize the steps it took to get to where they are, and instead, they picture that everything they earned was only because of luck.

Imposter syndrome destroys self-esteem. It can rob you of your confidence because you forget to acknowledge your success.

Types of Imposter Syndrome

Imposter syndrome can often turn people into perfectionists. As we already discussed in the previous section, perfectionism can be a temporary release for people who feel as though they don't have control over their lives.

The emotional outcome we experience can be debilitating and keep us trapped in a place of old trauma. Perfectionism can cause a person to struggle with feelings of control. You might be an individual that needs to have charge over a situation. Maybe you feel anxious if you are not the one who is in control.

Imposter syndrome can also lead people to be the type of individual who is seen as somebody almost like a superhero. These are often workaholics and those that exert themselves in areas that do not require so much excessive attention. This can be their method of making up for feelings of inadequacy.

Sometimes imposter syndrome might show up in individuals who feel like they have to be the expert. They might need to be somebody who is naturally intelligent with everything and completely independent. All of these types can turn somebody into an individual who is overworked and exhausted.

Maybe you're the type of individual who would rather get a task done and do it perfectly, rather than asking for help from others. Maybe you often notice yourself managing other people's lives and giving them advice while not being able to improve your own life. It's not that these thoughts you have about yourself are necessarily true, but imposter syndrome can make us feel that way.

Shift your attention towards your successes rather than weighing so heavily on your faults.

Factors Contributing to Imposter Syndrome

There are a few different reasons why somebody might struggle with imposter syndrome. Often, it's the way that we were raised. Those who had immense pressure placed on them as children likely struggle with the way they view themselves today. It can be very damaging to a child's self-esteem when they don't receive validation or acknowledgment for their success.

You might also have had parents who were perfectionists themselves. Maybe they had extremely high standards and would judge you. They might not have had those same judgments for themselves, and sometimes that can create a confusing perspective. You might have emotions that you don't understand and thoughts with no meaning because you're unable to recognize somebody else's mental health who raised you, let alone your own.

Many of the same factors that contribute to our feelings of perfectionism are intertwined with the reasons that we experience imposter syndrome.

Effects of Imposter Syndrome

The biggest effect of imposter syndrome is that it robs you of your self-esteem. To be confident, you have to be able to recognize your ability to succeed in an area. Imagine that you come to a river crossing your path and you have to jump over to the other side. If you have never jumped across the bridge before, would you have the confidence to do it now?

Maybe because you can look at past experiences and notice your success. You remember that time you jumped over a puddle or the time that you jumped on the stairs. Maybe you also remember times when you jumped and you fell. Instead of letting that defeat you, you can use your confidence to know that jumping isn't your strength, but maybe something else is.

Perhaps you can walk to a different area and find an easier place to step over, or maybe you can climb down a bit and cross the river safely.

Confidence takes your ability to reflect on past accomplishments and use that as energy to continue to push you forward. If you are blind to your success as those with imposter syndrome are, you never have that boost in the right direction. You're constantly going to be striving for more and always seeking out new validation to help accommodate these intense feelings of inadequacy that you're experiencing.

Avoiding and Overcoming Imposter Syndrome Exercises

Now that you know what imposter syndrome is, you might be asking, "How can I beat imposter syndrome?"

To overcome imposter syndrome, it all begins by taking a few steps in the right direction. You might have taken a while to build these habits up, but they can be broken down through repetition. You want to expose yourself to certain feelings and emotions as a reminder that your biggest fears dealing with confidence don't have to be factors that keep you hidden away from the world.

Admit You Were Wrong

One practical exercise you can do to overcome imposter syndrome is to practice what it feels like to admit you are wrong.

If you can reaffirm this with a person, especially a close friend, that can help you feel instantly relieved.

It's not easy to admit when we might have been wrong.

This isn't about just telling everybody that you're a horrible person or admitting to terrible things that you've done in the past. Admitting you're wrong is simply noticing moments when you weren't perfect and realizing that it's still okay.

Sometimes we don't admit we're wrong until we're caught with a lie. Maybe you were backed into the corner, and that's the only time you've admitted that you were wrong. Really, somebody with high confidence and who is successful has admitted they're wrong many times. It's the only way that you can improve on your mistakes. If you lie and cover it up or avoid your shortcomings, it just adds to the guilt you have about yourself. Admitting you're wrong is not admitting that you're a flawed person. That's not what this activity is about. The point is to realize that in those times when you might have been wrong, everything still turns out as it should. For this activity, do the following:

1. Pick out one thing you admitted you were wrong for in the past.

2. Pick out one thing that you should have admitted you were wrong for but never did.

3. Pick out another thing that you've kept hidden that only you know is wrong.

Reflect on these instances and recall how those situations made you feel and what you might be able to do now to remedy them. You don't have to spill all your secrets, but maybe sharing with others could validate your confidence by reminding you that people still love and appreciate you no matter what you've done. For example, maybe you cheated on a partner in the past but never told anyone and they never found out. You might tell a friend this to help get the secret off your chest and discover that you feel better about yourself afterward. Admitting it out loud helps to reaffirm that you know what you did wasn't great, giving you the chance to move on from this instance.

Participate in an Emotional Time Capsule

To participate in an emotional time capsule, it will involve writing yourself letters. This isn't just yourself now. You will address these letters to yourself at different time periods.

For your emotional time capsule, first, start by writing a letter to your past self. Share with them something you want to reflect on. Maybe you write a letter forgiving yourself. Perhaps you go back in time and relive a situation with a new perspective. Whatever you want to do, address a letter to your past self.

Now write a letter to your present self. What can you say to boost your confidence? Maybe you want to remind yourself that you're loved. Maybe you want to recognize that you are a beautiful person. What do you hope to gain from the future, and what do you think you should work on now?

Finally, write a letter to your future self. What do you hope to gain? Then ask, "What are you excited for?" What would be one thing that would make you really sad to find out you still do in the future.

These activities are just meant to help reflect in a way that makes you feel more authentic. You're having conversations with yourself and getting to know yourself a little bit better. We often forget that we still have a lot to learn about our own minds, and this activity will help you through that.

Fact-Check

Track your thoughts throughout the day. After the day has concluded, go back through and decide if each was a fact or an opinion.

We tell ourselves crazy things all throughout the day, and most of them are not true. These include the following phrases:

- "I can't do this."
- "I'm not good enough."
- "I'm ugly."
- "I'm a failure."

- "No one likes me."

For this fact-checking exercise, keep a notepad around you so you can quickly pull things out and write down your thoughts as needed. You don't have to confront them at this moment. You don't have to cure yourself of them. You don't need to feel the pressure to alleviate all the symptoms those thoughts might bring on.

Simply write them down and move on. Go back and use whatever statistics, research, or proof and evidence you have on this fact. For most of the opinions you have about yourself, you realize there is absolutely no evidence supporting that, making it easier to overcome those thoughts and brush them away as the simple opinions they are.

Chapter 7: Being Your Own Friend

Friendship is one of the greatest parts of life. There's nothing more comforting than knowing there are people out there who are interested in what you have to share with them. When we can connect with people who really see our personalities, it's one of the most fulfilling things we can experience.

Not everyone is lucky enough to have this kind of friendship based on the people in their life. However, this relationship is not one that is reserved for two people. It could be the relationship you have with yourself!

Becoming confident means that you truly love who you are. You will be able to look in the mirror and not only be content with what you see but also actively love the image staring back. You are the only person that you'll ever be, so you certainly deserve to have endless love for yourself.

By building this powerful skill individually, you'll be able to embrace who you truly are.

Self-Compassion Leads to Self-Acceptance

Being compassionate towards yourself is the first step towards accepting who you are. Self-compassion is when you are able to treat yourself in a way that you deserve. We all deserve to feel confident in our abilities and appreciate what we are capable of. The things we were taught to believe throughout our lives can get in the way of that, leaving you feeling as though you might deserve punishment, judgment, or negative treatment because of your actions and behaviors.

Self-compassion will eventually lead you towards accepting yourself.

You'll be able to appreciate who you are and be comfortable with any flaws or shortcomings you feel as though you possess. When you are compassionate towards yourself, you are kind and forgiving rather than judgmental and harsh.

If you fail a test, you might punish yourself by forcing yourself to study for hours over the weekend, missing out on fun activities. You might not even get much work done because you're so busy beating yourself up over the grade received. You might berate yourself and belittle your accomplishments, labeling yourself as dumb or incompetent based on the percentage of questions you got wrong on a singular test.

It's also important we recognize just how easily we can be our biggest bully. There are some people who might have actively harmed you that never hurt you quite as much as you've been able to hurt yourself.

You might judge yourself based on minor things like embarrassing jokes you say at a party or moments that you simply regret from your past. Self-compassion allows you to suspend some of that judgment. Instead of looking at these average flaws, you put focus on the positive aspects you might have added to somebody's life.

You'll be able to avoid holding a microscope against your flaws and, instead, zoom out so you can also see what benefits you have to offer.

Self-compassion changes the way that you see your body. It can reduce the stress you have over your successes or failures, and it makes you feel better about yourself in general. The best way to be self-compassionate is to treat yourself as though you are a loved one.

Treat Yourself as a Loved One

Imagine somebody that you love more than anything. They might have annoying moments or minor flaws, but you don't care at all. You love them unconditionally with no question through everything.

You might not be able to think of a person, and that's OK! Maybe you get annoyed easily by most people in your house. However, think about a pet, maybe even a celebrity or somebody that you really admire. There has to be at least one person that you don't have any sort of negative feelings towards. Now, imagine that this person is feeling very bad about themselves.

Envision a moment where they're next to you and they tell you that they believe they are disgusting, ugly, stupid, and/or worthless.

What would you say to them? You would likely tell them that's absurd and you would reassure them none of this is true. You remind them that you value them and that you appreciate them for everything. You'd show them why they were wrong and remind them they are valuable people that have a lot to offer.

This is exactly what you need to be telling yourself. Every time you look in the mirror and think something negative about your body, ask if that is the truth. Is this something that you've come to believe? Why do you have these thoughts and ideas, and what can you do to remedy them?

Imagine a friend that you enjoy spending time with. Think of a mistake they've made in their life that has nothing to do with you.

Do you think they deserve punishment for their mistakes? Do you believe you should treat them negatively because of the things they've done? Your answer is likely no. We are forgiving of people for their mistakes, even those that might have directly impacted us.

Be as forgiving to yourself. Let go of the regret and guilt that has been causing you to want to torture yourself. Maybe you feel like you've wasted years away. Perhaps you wish you could go back in time and pick a new college degree. Maybe it's the person you ended up with that you regret.

Whatever you want to turn the clock back on, think, if you were a friend, what would you tell them? You would remind them that everything is going to work out as it should. You let them know that you can't go back in time and that what they experienced has all helped develop them into the people they are now.

Treat yourself like somebody that you really love.

Part of loving somebody is taking responsibility for them. This is what you need to do now but for yourself. Recognize that your own happiness is in your control.

Self-responsibility involves accepting that you are the one who has power and who is in charge of what happens to you. There is nobody else who is going to tell you how to act or what you need to get done to live a happy life. You are the one in charge.

Self-Responsibility

There are a few important steps to take to be more responsible for yourself. The first is to stop casting blame on other people and yourself. There is no one who is directly at fault for everything that has occurred in your life. Of course, there are many individuals who have had influence, but they aren't necessarily directly in charge.

You might have been forced into a situation by someone else, but at the end of the day, it is your emotions that you still have power over. Blame for a situation means we also give someone else power over our emotions. You're letting them decide whether you'll be sad or happy.

Blaming someone for you being unhappy means it's easier to blame someone else when we act poorly. If you are angry and you yell at someone, it's easy to cast the blame on that person, not realizing that reaction only inhibits us in the long run.

This is important for your confidence because you want to recognize the power that you have over the ability to feel good about yourself and secure with your actions.

The Practice of Living Consciously

To be more responsible and compassionate, it's required that you are living in a conscious way. This includes being aware of how you talk to yourself and the way that you might also interact with your surroundings. Don't feel ashamed if you have been living mindlessly; most people do.

The first step to living more consciously is to look at the core truth or the big picture of a situation. Don't just get glued to the minor details and stay magnetized to a false perception. Admit to yourself when you might be ignoring the truth and become more aware of times when you might turn your cheek to reality.

Pay attention to common and frequent distractions. What often pulls you from being able to pay attention to your surroundings? Is it your thoughts that keep your brain stuck in a different place? Notice these aspects to become more aware of all that surrounds you. This is similar to mindful living, but rather than just being present of your thoughts, you want to pay attention to how you're influencing and affecting others as well. Let's take a look at some exercises that can aid in your ability to live a more conscious life.

Self-Love Exercises

These self-love exercises are going to bring you one step closer to enjoying the skin that you're in. You're going to want to try to find that healthy relationship to keep yourself living and flourishing consistently in life. The more that you normalize self-compassion, the easier it will be to forgive yourself for your mistakes.

Help Others

Sometimes when you give to someone else, it can boost your confidence and make you feel better about yourself. By helping other people, it makes it easier for you to be compassionate, allowing you to have that same love for yourself.

Helping people doesn't just mean that you go to a soup kitchen every weekend. Think of small ways to help others. Maybe you bring coffee in for your coworker. Perhaps you clean the apartment even though it was your roommate who was messy.

Resenting, loathing, and even hating other people can make us internalize that anger and have those same feelings for ourselves. Free yourself from this and, instead, give yourself the opportunity to be selfish for a moment by giving to others to make yourself feel more confident.

Practice Saying "No"

Stop putting people before yourself and begin to strengthen your voice. Saying no can be uncomfortable in some situations, especially if you fear people are going to not like you anymore.

If anyone dislikes you because of your ability to stand up for yourself, you shouldn't be concerned about having them in your life anyway!

You can't give from an empty cup, so allow yourself to say no when you need to. For this activity, come up with three scenarios that might cause you to feel pressured to say yes when you want to say no. Then come up with three responses for each as to how you can politely and directly say no so that you are prepared when this situation might occur.

Self-Gratitude

Part of having gratitude for yourself will also include being thankful for the mistakes you might have made or other things you experienced throughout your life.

Gratitude is all about showing appreciation for the things in life. This includes everything from what is obviously a great life addition to even things that aren't so great.

For example, you could be grateful for getting fired because that led you to a new job where you ended up meeting your wife!

Practice gratitude every single day. Take five minutes out of your day to reflect on things you are grateful for. This might include the following:

- People in your life (even enemies who have taught you something about yourself or people who have become examples of how you DON'T want to live your life)

- Functions of your body (the ability to walk, see, talk, eat, etc.)
- Material possessions
- Freedoms (running water, electricity, freedom of speech, etc.)
- Experiences (getting an education, family parties, etc.)
- Food and entertainment
- Nature and the beauty of the world (flowers, waterfalls, animals, etc.)

There is always at least one thing to be grateful for, and the more you notice this, the easier it will be to alleviate anxiety, therefore increasing confidence.

Chapter 8: What Doesn't Work

There are some myths about building confidence that need to be addressed. The idea that confidence is a singular act or that it's a natural trait keeps us feeling like we can't be confident when we don't fit the right mold. By adopting a healthier mindset and avoiding the things below, you can put the view you have of yourself in reverse and adopt a new, productive mindset (Selig, 2018).

People have likely told you before to just be more positive, maybe through the use of motivational quotes. That could work at first, but if you're not using them in the right way, it can fall through. We're also told that criticism or comparing ourselves in a competitive way can be what motivates us to propel forward. Alcohol, drugs, and other vices can fall into our lives naturally and cause destruction over our lives. By avoiding these and turning your attention instead to the activities at the end, you'll be able to focus on living a happy and healthier life much easier, filled with confidence.

Positive Affirmations

The first thing that doesn't quite work for everybody is the use of positive affirmations. An affirmation is any sort of statement of truth. People use positive affirmations in a repetitive way to help instill a new belief. On the one hand, these could work because they help to confront cognitive distortions. If you're constantly thinking to yourself negative thoughts like "I'm the worst," "I can't do it," "I'm a terrible person," you can start to replace those with positive affirmations.

However, these don't work because too many people simply state them out loud. They put signs around their house or they use them in their captions for social media, but they don't actually work if you're not putting the right mindset behind that.

To use a positive affirmation, first, you have to confront the negative one that you're trying to overcome. You have to acknowledge what is already being repeated in your head. You also have to believe in those affirmations.

You can't just say, "I'm a good person," if you truly don't see how you're a good person. Before using those affirmations, you want to go through and find the legitimacy behind them to make them more efficient.

If you want to use a positive affirmation, start by finding a simple mantra.

Notice what you're saying now that is keeping you held back. Do you often look in the mirror and think, "I'm ugly"? Do you feel like you can't complete things and you always tell yourself, "I can't do this"? Maybe you struggle because you tell yourself that you're not good enough.

Whatever these thoughts and opinions that you consistently share may be, you can begin to confront them in a healthy way. Positive affirmations only assist you when dealing with cognitive distortions or other negative thoughts. They are not the elixir to negativity, simply the bottle that it is held in.

Alcohol, Drugs, and Other Vices

One thing that certainly does not work for confidence is drugs, alcohol, and any other sort of vices. These things provide temporary relief, but that's about it. Eventually, that fades and no longer are those feelings of confidence present.

Many people like that liquid courage that alcohol can provide. It's easy to take a drink and suddenly feel more confident. If you do this every once in a while for maybe a date, of course, there's no harm in that. However, if this becomes a crutch and like a medicine, that's when it becomes a challenge. The same thing can be said for those who use drugs. Something like marijuana can help numb the pain of being so insecure. It might reduce that stress and anxiety that keeps you feeling like you have no confidence whatsoever. Just like getting drunk, the high will still wear off, leaving you feeling worse than before you took the substance.

These things only provide temporary relief. Eventually, that fades, and those feelings of insecurity come back once again. It's like putting makeup on an infected wound. If you're not actually treating the infection, it's only going to get worse, even if you can't see it.

Sometimes people use things like sex or food to also numb the pain. Remember that all these things might be fine on a smaller basis. You can enjoy a few drinks with friends. You can eat food that you know is bad for you but in a small amount. It's when you're doing these things in excess and as a requirement for basic standards of living that it becomes a huge issue.

Comparison

Another thing that really doesn't work to help improve how we feel about ourselves is constant comparison. Comparison happens everywhere. It's on social media, and it's on TV. It's in our phones. It's in our own homes. We compare ourselves to everybody and everything, but most of the time, this is done in a very unfair way.

It leaves us feeling completely hopeless and lost because we aren't comparing ourselves in a realistic way. Let's take social media for example. It's easy to go online and see a million people who are very happy. They'll talk about all their family's accomplishments, and they'll go on about the good things they did that day. What they don't show you are many of the struggles. Of course, everybody likes to have moments where they might "get real" or open up and be vulnerable on social media, but they don't show the really bad stuff.

They don't show that they might not have that much money in their bank account. They're not sharing with you that they're struggling to know how to pay their bills. They're not going to discuss their child's behavior problems at school. They might not be willing to open up about a crazy in-law or a toxic ex they keep going back to.

These things are very real and can happen to any of us, and they might feel defeated. It might be a reason that we use to validate the insecurities we have about ourselves.

When we make those comparisons, we judge ourselves based on the fact that the other person does not have our shortcomings. We can't say that's true. We only compare other people's good parts with our bad parts, and it leaves us feeling hopeless and lost.

Comparison can help in some ways. If you're trying to create certain standards of understanding, maybe you compare your workload with somebody else's to see if you're working efficiently. A co-worker might be able to complete 10 tasks in the time it takes you to complete 6. You can compare their quality too. Maybe they finish their tasks as high quality as you are. This then can give you a sign that you should try to work more efficiently. The reflection should be done in a healthy way that encourages you, not one that makes you feel like you're a failure compared to the other person.

Avoid comparison as often as possible because often you're going to be doing it in a way that is unfair to your self-esteem. Sometimes it happens naturally, and there are a few circumstances it can help, but for the most part, it is just going to keep you trapped in a place where you constantly feel bad about yourself.

Self-Criticism

The final thing that doesn't really work that well is self-criticism.

It's easy to want to criticize yourself. You might look in the mirror and easily be able to come up with a million insults that you can say. However, these often leave us feeling like we have very low self-esteem. It makes us feel bad about ourselves and like we are not worthy of the world around us.

Don't let this become your normal. Give yourself the ability to see your benefits. You can criticize yourself in a way that might be more constructive. Perhaps you admit to yourself that you didn't work as hard as you knew you could, or you might have lied to a friend or told a half-truth to a spouse. Be critical and reflective of these things that you know deep down are bad, but don't over-criticize yourself. If you can't decide where the line is, see what you would criticize in another person. You'd likely admit that not doing any work for five days in a row isn't healthy, but if they wanted to leave work half an hour early, that wouldn't be a big deal. Hold yourself to the same standards you hold others.

You need to use just as more positive encouragement than you do negative.

There's nothing wrong with making yourself feel good. Many people think that if they're harsh on themselves, that's just being self-aware. That's not the case at all!

To be truly self-aware, you recognize the good and the bad, and you treat yourself in a compassionate and loving way. Remind yourself that you're strong enough to power through your weaknesses and use your strengths as an encouragement to continue pushing forward.

Some people feel like encouraging themselves or using compassion is going to make them arrogant, so they use criticism instead. Again, this is not doing anyone any good! In fact, it's only going to keep you trapped in a place where you truly dislike yourself. Why would you want to do anything good for yourself if you consistently dislike who you are? No one is going to go that far out of their way to take good care of an individual they loathe. Instead, build that loving and trusting relationship with yourself so you have the energy and encouragement needed to get things done.

Simple Daily Exercises

You might have been using alcohol and drugs in a negative way. Perhaps you constantly compare yourself to others and criticize everything that you do. This doesn't have to be your new normal for behavior; instead, you can replace those ideas with something good.

These daily exercises can replace and replenish what damage bad habits have been doing in your life. Rather than focusing on what works for other people, pay attention to what works for you.

Pleasure Activities

Find something that you absolutely adore. Whatever it is that you like doing, find a structured time on a weekly basis to do this.

If you like running, biking, or other forms of exercise, that's perfect.

If you enjoy watching TV and sitting on the couch, that's fine too. The point is to discover an activity that can be your "me" time. This is one specific thing that you will give to yourself on a weekly basis, completely free from other people.

Try to remove yourself from the concept that you have to feel guilty over certain things you're doing. Whatever your "guilty" pleasure might be, make that a regular pleasure — even if it's eating ice cream. Schedule this time weekly because it is just as important as things like work or meetings that we schedule. Don't make yourself feel guilty for doing things that you enjoy in life.

Fake a Smile

It sounds uncomfortable, but if you fake a smile throughout the day, it can trick your brain into thinking you are happy (Kraft & Pressman, 2012).

Having confidence won't always equate to not being afraid. Confidence, faking smiles, and everything else you do for an esteem boost is a reminder that even though you're scared, you are strong enough to overcome your greatest fears.

When you're stressed or anxious, smile or laugh in the mirror for a few minutes to help trick your mind. It's not going to cure depression instantly, but it can help boost your mood at least a little to momentarily increase your ability to be mindful and work through those emotions.

Emotion-Focused Coping

When a situation can't be changed, you can begin to use emotion-focused coping.

Whenever there is a problem that needs to be solved, most individuals will look at how to fix that issue. This would be considered problem-focused coping. This is perfect for family fights or workplace drama.

However, what do you do when you feel as though you are constantly trying to fix something but never getting any good results? That is where emotion-focused coping can come into play. The point of this activity is to help you identify how you can overcome the emotions connected to a problem rather than finding its solution.

Sometimes it is not a solution that the situation needs but rather an entirely new perspective. For example, let's say that you hate your job. You can't stand waking up for work in the morning, and the entire time you sit behind your office desk, you are miserable. You applied to a ton of other jobs, but none of them pay as much, and you just haven't had the best luck hearing back in general. Problem-focused coping didn't and isn't going to help because none of the solutions presented worked. Now it is time for you to look at emotion-focused coping (Scott, 2019).

These are strategies that are very similar to what we've been discussing, like confronting cognitive distortions or journaling.

One of the simplest ways to turn these emotions around is through reframing. The problem in this situation is no longer that you should get a new job. You could go back to school and start over. You could move to a different city and find something more high-paying. You could take your chances with the lottery.

None of these are absolute or quick solutions, so you want to use cognitive reframing to come up with a new way to cope.

To start to do this, ask yourself questions like these:

- "Who would be an individual that might be envious of my position?"
- "Are there others who wish they were in my position now?"
- "What would I lose to make this situation worse?"
- "How has this situation been an improvement in another area of my life?"
- "What can I do to be more positive about this situation?"
- "How can I learn to be appreciative of this scenario?"

To keep going with the job example, you can answer the first two questions easily. There are plenty of people who are unemployed or making the very minimum who would kill for a higher-paying position. There are likely people in your office who are envious of your work and would love a job like that. If you were to quit, someone would come in and take your job, so they would go through the same things.

What is preventing you from being able to enjoy this position? By doing deep reflection, you can realize that it's not the scenario that needs to change but simply your mindset.

Chapter 9: Leaving Your Comfort Zone with Exposure and Repetition for Confidence

Cognitive behavioral therapy is a groundbreaking method of mental training to confront the cognitive distortions that plague your mind and, instead, build a healthier and more functioning thought process. Since its development in the '60s, it has only become more effective for treating mental health disorders, such as anxiety, depression, and obsessive-compulsive disorder.

It is not a therapy that requires medication, but the assistance of a professional can help effectiveness increase. Regardless of whether you struggle with a severe mental disorder or you just want to increase your cognitive function, there are many benefits to be discovered from CTB techniques.

Cognitive Behavioral Therapy

CBT is one of the best methods to control your anxiety. It allows you to tackle these feelings head-on.

To fully understand what cognitive-behavioral therapy is, let's start by breaking down the acronym. First is "cognitive." This refers to any way that your brain thinks.

One of the most important aspects of understanding your cognitive functions is recognizing what your fight-or-flight response is. Some of us won't truly know how we would react until we come face-to-face with an immense threat such as an attack.

But we do still have minor instances of this reaction on a daily basis. When you are exposed to new threats, you will respond either in a fight or flight fashion. If somebody starts yelling at you because they're angry, you might fight them back, or you might avoid them and walk away from the scenario.

You might also use flight instincts in this situation by reverting inwards and rejecting to listen to them. Cognitive function also refers to the thoughts that you consistently stick to.

Are you always going over thoughts of the past? Are you afraid of everything that's about to happen? Where do your thoughts go, and what emphasis is placed on the ideas that passed in and out of your brain?

The second word is "behavior." How do these thoughts in all parts of your cognition affect the way that you interact in the world? Some people are perfectly fine by managing their emotions, and they don't ever have any problems that affect them or the outside world. Others struggle because their thoughts constantly take away from their ability to live a happy life.

Therapy refers to how we can begin to confront these emotions and ideas and turn them into beneficial feelings.

To fully grasp how cognitive behavioral therapy works, let's take a look at some basic techniques that CBT can help to overcome.

CBT Techniques

Many of the activities we covered in this chapter can be considered CBT activities. These include the following:

- Journaling
- Mindfulness
- Confronting cognitive distortions

Cognitive behavioral therapy often deals with anything that greatly impacts our minds or our thoughts. This can include something like anxiety or depression. These can be genetic, and they are chemical processes that occur, not always just behavioral. Our patterns of thought can also be something that developed over time. This can still be remedied with the use of CBT because of one's ability to overcome the patterns of thought that keep them trapped in the same ways of thinking.

Any addictions or eating disorders can also be remedied with the help of cognitive behavioral therapy. Something like addiction or eating disorders are patterns of behavior that are affected by various mental thoughts. Cognitive behavioral therapy can assist with this by confronting the feelings that cause the behavior. One of the techniques to understand this is tracing thoughts back. This is referred to in CBT as unraveling.

When unraveling, you look at these thoughts, and you go back to where they began. If you believe that you are worthless or lazy, maybe that's because your stepfather used to tell you that you are worthless or lazy. If you believe you are ugly, it could be that somebody in your life told you over and over again you're ugly. It could be a constant romantic rejection. It could be a number of factors.

Instead of looking at those factors, some people will simply try to confront the feeling. Now, that doesn't always help because the underlying issue isn't being addressed. You might be called ugly by just your father, and everybody else in life thinks that you are absolutely beautiful. You use that validation of other people's opinions to help you feel better about yourself. However, that true fulfillment is never achieved because it's not about you believing that you're ugly; it's about not getting that kind of approval from your father. He placed such an emphasis on calling you ugly that it developed your own emphasis on looks in general. He thought it was important enough to tell you that you were ugly; therefore, you grew to believe that looks were very important. You never got his approval; therefore, you didn't fulfill this importance in your mind. The true issue can only be discovered if we dive into our deep cognitive and behaviors.

CBT involves techniques that are all about coming face to face with the most deeply rooted cause for your behavior.

If you are weeding a garden, you don't chop off the weeds at the top because they keep growing back. You want to dig out the root and clean that area out to ensure that they never come back. This is why CBT techniques are often short and simple in process, but the effect can be much longer.

Those who practice CBT also discover they don't need to go to therapy for decades. They can overcome these feelings in weeks or months, depending on the issue that they're attacking.

CBT is all about taking small steps.

Small Steps

Small steps are important because they are how the beginning gets easier. If you're sitting there trying to figure out how to overcome an eating disorder that you've had since junior high, that's extremely overwhelming. The eating disorder has become a natural part of you, and it's how you function in the world. It's the way that you perceive your surroundings, and it likely creates patterns of judgment. To think that all of a sudden, you have to change your life completely overnight can be the very thing that drives you back into a place of high anxiety. You don't have to cure yourself right away, and that is where CBT can really come in to make this transition a little easier.

Small steps are also important because that is how you will overcome gradual change. Let's say that you wanted to lose weight. Would you want to do it in a way that takes you a few years and helps you go through it naturally, or would you crash-diet to try to do it all within a month? You could accomplish that goal within a month, but you haven't been able to develop long-term healthy habits. It's easy to then revert right back to your old ways of eating, resulting in weight gain.

You can go through this quickly if you like, but it's not going to be like a Band-Aid getting ripped off.

You can attack it from an intense place right from the beginning, but remember that to truly see the long-term results, it's going to take time, and that is all done through small steps.

Small steps forward mean that any steps backward aren't as hard to overcome. The higher you climb, the farther you fall. The farther you fall, the harder you fall.

If you were to do this too quickly and expose yourself to your anxieties in a place that is overwhelming, it might revert you straight back into the same mindset you had when you experienced the trauma.

For example, let's say that you were abused as a child by your father. Perhaps you haven't spoken to him in a decade, and after a month of building your confidence and working through, you might decide you want to visit your father. You visit him, and then you realize you aren't prepared, and it becomes another new traumatic experience that could have been avoided had you waited until you are actually ready. Small steps will help you be more careful in this process to keep your confidence protected the entire time. Having high self-esteem is only going to aid and make things easier in general.

Fear of Rejection and Bullying

Cognitive behavioral therapy can help us with any feelings of rejection and bullying. This is important for confidence building and is one area that we really want to focus on for this book. Your confidence is something that might have been taken away by somebody else in the past. This could have been because of bullying, or it might have just been the way that a father or mother talked about you.

Fear of rejection can prevent us from doing things that we know are good for us. It provides us with this intense paranoia that, if we fail, we are not as good as our shortcomings.

Cognitive behavioral therapy helps you to work through those fears and realize that they aren't things you need to be so paranoid about. You might fail, and you might get rejected, but that doesn't have to be the scary thing that you've come to believe it is. Instead, it can be something that helps you overcome your deepest insecurities in the end.

Embrace failure and allow yourself not to fear making any mistakes. Failure is a natural part of life, and it's important to begin to look at it in this way. Failure allows us to recognize that what we did was wrong to ensure that we will never do it again.

Whenever you cook, you're likely cautious in an average way. It is only until you burn the house down from cooking that you realize how to be especially cautious. When we live through that mistake, we become equipped with the knowledge of just how much we never want to live through that again. It can be a powerful and scary feeling for some, but it also provides us with a reminder of just how much we have to fight for.

Exposure Therapy Exercises

Exposure to the things that cause you anxiety can help to increase your chances of finding effectiveness.

Of course, this isn't always the case, so be cautious also with how you go about participating in these therapies. Sometimes too much exposure too early on can cause you to be just as panicked as you were when you might have experienced initial trauma. Instead, focus on gradually easing into this process and try out some of these light exposure activities to help manage your anxiety and boost confidence.

Body Posture

Amy Cuddy is a social psychologist who conducted a study on how your body posture can affect the mood you have (Cuddy, 2012). By adopting certain poses, it becomes easier to elicit feelings of confidence.

From the top of your head all the way down to your feet, you could be giving off signs that you lack confidence. This can feed into your mentality, making you feel trapped and hopeless. Start to break that down to enable yourself to fit in with the situation around you better.

The first thing to notice is how you are holding your posture. Where are your shoulders and neck? By sitting up straight and opening your shoulders, you are already boosting your confidence.

Keep your chin tilted up as well. That is not to look down your nose at other people, but most of us are tucked in, to the point that we are recoiling and hiding from those around us. Don't do this! It only makes you seem more afraid, and that can change how people treat you, leading to even more feelings of a lack of confidence.

Keep your arms and legs open as well. Sometimes you might have to sit with your legs crossed to make the situation more comfortable, but other than reasons of necessity, check in to make sure you aren't keeping yourself totally closed off from the outside world.

Make sure not to fidget and keep your hands out of your pockets. When you hide your hands away, not only does it make you look more afraid, but it also can make you seem untrustworthy.

Of course, avoiding fidgeting isn't easy. Most of us don't even realize we're doing it. That is where breathing exercises and mindfulness are going to help you the most. If you notice yourself picking at your fingers, shaking your leg, or messing around with objects in front of you, take a breath and notice your surroundings. It might happen again in as little as a few minutes, but consistency is the key to breaking down these issues.

You can start to change someone else's body language to boost your confidence further. You can stand up over them during a meeting, making yourself seem bigger. This could be enough to give the illusion you're more confident than you are. If someone is closed off, mimic their body language for a moment. If they're hunched over with their arms crossed, do the same thing. After a couple of minutes, sit up straight and stretch your arms out.

There's a good chance that within a few minutes, they will do the same.

You can try handing something to another person to also help your ability to open them up just a bit. Maybe you give the interviewer your résumé or someone else a glass of water to keep them from crossing their arms or closing off.

Focus on your body and how it might be interpreted within a space to get a greater understanding of how you might be affecting the perception that others have of you.

Finding What You're Good At

This practical exercise is to help remind you of what your real worth is.

You might know a few things you're good at already. Maybe you're good at some video games you have, or you like to draw. Go beyond just physical things that you do with your hand.

Find what you are good at emotionally. How do you change the world? What is it that you have that can affect others in a positive way?

To determine what you're good at, first, look at one thing that makes you feel really good about yourself. This doesn't have to be what you're perfect at, but pick out something that you legitimately enjoy. How does this activity affect others? How does it enhance your life?

If you can't answer these two questions, you might enjoy something that's not great for you. For example, you might really enjoy drinking alcohol. Maybe it's your favorite thing to do. Does it help improve the lives of others when you drink? Does it improve your life?

This isn't to demonize alcohol either. However, what you're good at should be something that can enable you to thrive. If you legitimately like drinking but don't do excessively, there could be a hobby there! Maybe you get into making extravagant cocktails, or you start to experiment with brewing your own beer or wine. Eventually, you could start selling this or maybe even open your own brewery one day.

Pay attention to what others tell you that you are good at. Really listen to the areas of your life that you receive the most compliments.

Sometimes we don't even realize that we already have an intense set of skills. Maybe you're great at cooking, but you don't really see yourself as that extraordinary. Perhaps other people frequently tell you that you are a good cook, so you can use this to realize you are a little different from the rest.

Remember to look at this emotionally as well. Do you help other people? Maybe you're good at giving advice or showing support as a friend. When you determine what you are good at, you are reflecting on yourself in a healthy way. You're taking the chance to understand that you are a valuable person with plenty of skills to offer the world.

Find a Support System

There are many research-backed reasons that you should find a support system. It helps to make you feel better, keep you accountable, and open avenues that you might not be able to explore on your own.

The first kind of support system to find through your confidence recovery is someone close to you that you can talk to about whatever deep issues you're having. Tell this person that you are actively going to be working on yourself to make them aware of the severity of this position you've given them.

Come up with moments of reflection together. This is great for best friends, romantic partners, or siblings. You can both work on these issues together and hold one another accountable. You can challenge each other in different ways. Maybe you have a jar that you each have to put money in whenever you say something negative about yourself out loud. This support system makes this process much more realistic. You're able to see that you have someone else going through the same thing, reminding you that this is a normal process and not one you have to be afraid of being a part of.

The second kind of support system is one that's more professional. This could be a therapist or doctor that you go to in order to discuss your issues with confidence. You can share with them that you're having trouble overcoming your constant doubt or worry. They might even be able to diagnose you with something like depression or OCD that can be remedied with more specific therapies.

You should seek out group support systems if possible. This could be a group therapy session on body image issues. If you are a woman, there are many female-oriented group therapies for those who struggle with confidence. If you struggle with eating disorders or addiction, you can also seek out group therapy to be that support system to hold you accountable and offer help when needed.

You can also consider finding online support. There are endless communities on the internet you can discover to help you rant, vent, and go online to not be afraid to share your thoughts anonymously. Places like Reddit, Tumblr, and other social media platforms can be places to have discussions with those going through similar things.

Don't be afraid to reach out and talk about your issues. It could be the very thing you need to begin to increase your confidence.

Chapter 10: How Meditation Can Improve Your Self-Esteem

Meditation has been around for an unrecordable time. Meditation might not have always carried that term, but this method of relaxation has been an off-the-books treatment for many anxious minds before science started to discover its legitimacy.

Meditation is going to be a great way for you to increase the way you see yourself. Rather than being uncomfortable in your skin with a swirling and anxious mind, you can become more relaxed and at ease with the person you are now.

Meditation Is the Key to Self-Control

Meditation is one of the best ways you can start to improve your overall self-control. Throughout the day, you might just be guided by your wants and desires. Maybe you eat when you want to, you get on your phone when you want to, and you procrastinate work or other tasks and choose to do fun things instead.

It's good to do what you want on some level, but we also require self-discipline for success. Sometimes you need to be reminded to work out or clean the house. Meditation can help increase that control inside of you. It reminds you that you have to get things done, and you don't really have a choice some of the time. It teaches you how to manage your emotions properly so these things are easier to have control over.

Stress can be a motivation, but not when it's so high that we lose sight of reality. Stress can cause us to become panicked or overwhelmed. You might not be able to think clearly to know exactly what you have to do to get things done.

Meditation is also really good for you because it helps you better manage stress. You'll be able to confront those hard feelings of panic or anxiety and be reminded that everything is going to be okay. Instead of wasting hours ruminating in anxious thoughts, you can come up with a clear plan for what needs to get done and tackle the most important tasks.

Because of your stress reduction, you might also find that it's easier to manage anger. Meditation somewhat resets the mind. All day long, we keep going and going throughout the motions, often multitasking or getting easily distracted. When you meditate, you give your brain the chance to get into reset mode.

It has this ability to power down for just a moment so it can come back refreshed and rejuvenated. Whenever you use your brain to actively think, it requires a little more energy.

When you're sleeping, your brain has a chance to relax just a bit, but that doesn't mean that you stopped thinking. Our brain never turns off; it's always going. If we don't give it that chance to really relax and rest, it will always be on high energy. You might always be anxious, stressed, and worried because your brain feels incredibly overwhelmed.

Calm your mind through meditation and free your brain from these overwhelming thoughts.

The point of meditation is to suspend your thoughts. Anytime you do have an idea, panic, or worry come into your brain, you should gently push it out. It's not about repressing these emotions that are making yourself feel guilty for having them. The point is to refocus your mind and make it easier to move on to the next subject.

Studies on Meditation

Meditation is scientifically proven to help increase stress management. Research shows that meditation is one of the most effective ways to manage your thoughts and feelings without medication or other treatments. Studies have been conducted on various groups to see how meditation can affect their daily life. The general consensus is that people who meditate at least once a week have improved health, decreased stress, and increased emotional management.

Part of this can simply be acknowledging that your emotions do need to be managed and taking an active role beyond just meditation to help you work through those thought processes.

Meditation isn't just sitting in silence. You can practice guided meditation throughout different times of the day, such as in the morning or before bed. Exercises like yoga can also be considered meditation, depending on how you do them.

Meditation can also increase your attention span and boost your memory.

Over 12 studies have been conducted to help determine the effects of meditation on some of the negative aspects of aging and found that it can help increase focus and memory. Meditation can also help increase our ability to be kind to one another. It might help you manage your blood pressure, therefore leading to benefits related to heart health. Anything that can increase not just your mental health but also your physical health is an activity to be sought out (Thorpe, 2017).

Meditation Exercises

Meditation is easy and something that anyone can practice. However, that doesn't mean it's going to be simple at first for everyone. With these beginner exercises, you'll be able to practice long-form meditation in no time. Remember to keep an open mind and willingness to confront thoughts to begin meditation.

Creating a Meditative Space

The best thing you can do for meditation is to create your own specific meditation space. Our mind has muscle memory, which means when you get into a situation, sometimes it's easy to switch into autopilot.

Think of the last time that you drove home from work, only to realize you don't actually remember driving home all the way. It's such a repetitive activity that you can do it subconsciously while you think and let your mind drift to other areas.

Maybe you've sat on the couch and watched TV, only to realize that you ate through an entire bag of chips without realizing it. Your brain snaps back into the same mindset that is associated with a specific location.

This means you can train your brain to snap into a sort of relaxed composition depending on where you put your body physically to meditate. You want to create a specific space that's dedicated only to meditation. This would involve something like a carved-out location in a garden. Maybe you have a separate room for meditating.

You might not have a very big space at all. Perhaps you live in a studio apartment and there's already not enough room as there is. You don't have to cultivate an entire area. Simply pick out one spot that you do nothing else in.

If you pick to sit at the same place where you work, for example, you can click your mindset into work mode. Then you'll become stressed because you think of all these issues relating to your job.

Instead, pick somewhere that you don't do anything whatsoever. Again, if you were to sit on the couch where you normally watch TV, your brain might snap into that autopilot mode where it just wants to turn on the TV.

Even if it's something like the opposite end of your couch or the space at the end of your bed, you can still find one singular spot in your home that you don't do anything else in. You might even just sit in the middle of the kitchen floor. Of course, the kitchen can be associated with a lot of things, but if you sit in a specific way in a location that you aren't often traveling or walking through, it can still be a nice peaceful relaxation. Then when you're stressed out and you need to meditate, you can seek this location out, and hopefully, your brain will start to form into that peaceful mind on its own.

Beginner Meditation

To start a meditation session, make sure that you sit comfortably. There are a few different positions that you can sit in. One involves placing the bottom of your feet together and pulling your heels in towards your groin as close as you can. You'll sit up straight and then keep your hands placed on either knee.

If you are planning on doing something after you meditate, this is a good position to be in so that you don't get too sleepy. Instead, you'll just be relaxed and focused. You can also choose to meditate by lying down. You can lie in a bed, or you can lie on something like a yoga mat.

Meditation doesn't typically involve standing up because it might be hard for you to concentrate, but you could try something like this if you're just doing a quick meditation, perhaps outside near your garden or something like that.

Focus on your breathing.

Meditation is all about paying attention to the air that comes in and out of your body. To breathe in a relaxed way during meditation, it's easy to start by breathing in through your nose and out through your mouth. Don't force it and don't hold your breath for too long. Gently pull air in through both nostrils, and then gently let it come out through your mouth. You don't have to do this mouth-nose altering the entire time, but it can help you get focused at the beginning.

Count your breaths in whatever way you feel comfortable, usually between 3 and 10. That means you might breathe in as you count 1, 2, and 3, or you might breathe in as you count down from 10. You should not feel rushed. Counting while focusing on your breathing can help your brain concentrate.

Every time a thought comes into your head, simply push it away. Don't try to confront it. Don't try to solve it, and don't try to suppress it; let it pass through. Imagine you are sitting on the side of the street. Each time a car passes, it represents one of your thoughts. You don't want to go and stand in the middle of the street and let the car hit you. You're not going to stop the car or flag down the driver.

You're just simply watching those thoughts pass on by.

You might only be able to meditate for 30 seconds at first. Eventually, you can get into a place where you are meditating for up to 30 minutes or more. There are plenty of meditation scripts and audio recordings online that you can use, and YouTube is filled with hundreds of free guided meditations that you can play while you sit and relax.

Yoga Breathing

Breathing is a great way to stay focused and pull you back into a space of a healthy mindset. To do this, make a fist with your hand. Stick your thumb and your pinky out.

If you're right-handed, start with your right hand. If you're left-handed, do the opposite of what we say going forward. Now, take your right thumb and place it on your right nostril.

Breathe in deeply through your left nostril, keeping your mouth closed. Count to five. Hold it for one.

As you hold your breath, take your right pinky and then place it on your left nostril. Now breathe out through your right nostril as you lift your thumb up.

It's one quick motion switching from pinky to thumb. Do this until you feel relaxed and then switch to the opposite hand to help change things up a bit. You can include this in your meditation practice and do it beforehand, or you can just do it whenever you need it when you're feeling a little anxious.

Self-Hypnosis

There's one self-hypnosis trick you can use to snap you into the right mentality whenever needed. It's a mindfulness tactic that makes it easier for you to focus on the present moment. To start, pay attention to your breathing just as you would with regular meditation.

Next, look up using only your eyes and not your neck.

Pretend that you are looking at your eyebrows, and make your eyes go as deep up as you possibly can into your eye sockets. Don't close your eyes and don't tilt your head.

As you look up, breathe in and count to five. Continue looking up and only breathe in as you count. It's going to be a huge breath. Once you reach one, let it all out, look ahead of you, and snap your fingers. This is all done at once.

It's a way that instantly pulls you back into the moment. It might be uncomfortable, and you might even feel a little dizzy or lightheaded afterward. That's normal.

Anything too extreme is a sign you went too hard. Be careful because that could actually tense your muscles and cause physical pain. When done properly, this is still a great activity that will work when you're extremely stressed and nothing is seeming to calm you down.

The end... almost!

Reviews are not easy to come by.

As an independent author with a tiny marketing budget, I rely on readers, like you, to leave a short review on Amazon.

Even if it's just a sentence or two!

So if you enjoyed the book, please...

>> Scan here to leave a brief review on Amazon.

I am very appreciative for your review as it truly makes a difference.

Thank you from the bottom of my heart for purchasing this book and reading it to the end.

Conclusion

A lack of confidence is caused by a lack of an ability to believe in yourself. Whenever you feel that you're not capable of something, or that you're not good enough, it can stem back to a deeper underlying issue in your brain.

None of us are just born naturally hating ourselves. We don't come out of the womb instantly disliking the person that we are. Throughout time and different experiences, we are taught to feel this way. If you struggle with your confidence, you likely struggle with your anxiety. That is why, through this book, we have provided you with so many mindfulness activities and methods of working through those deep underlying emotions.

It might have felt like a deep, emotional journey throughout this book, and that's good. It should feel that way.

Confidence isn't just looking in the mirror and faking a smile every day. Yes, of course, that is one of the activities that we suggested, and it can help you to trick your brain into thinking you are temporarily happy. The point is, this is not a one-activity fix.

There's no quick solution or button you can press in your mind to make you confident. It's a skill that will take time to build and that you have to improve on with different methods of practice. Any of these activities is not going to cure your issues with confidence. It is a combination of many to tackle the deep and intrinsic underlying issues that cause you to have debilitating fear. Whether you were raised in a home that killed your spirit or you had a bad relationship recently that destroyed your confidence, you can get it back!

It is something that you will be able to grow and prosper as you continue throughout life on this crazy anxiety-inducing adventure.

Sometimes people become afraid that they're going to be too confident. What if you get a big head or become arrogant?

The thing is, those are not the same things as having true confidence. You might be full of yourself, you might think you've done nothing wrong, and you might believe that you are better than other people. None of those characteristics are inclusive of somebody who has true confidence and high self-esteem.

You might be able to get up and stand in front of a crowd, but when you're at home alone in bed or looking in the mirror, your true feelings will come out. That tells all.

When we're around other people, sometimes we can click into the right mindset. If you were raised as a pageant queen or somebody who is always cast in the spotlight, there's a good chance you have the ability to be brave in front of others. It might not be a huge issue for you to give speeches or be performative.

That doesn't mean that you're comfortable with yourself or that you're satisfied with who you are. At the end of the day, it is you who is alone, lying in bed. Even if you have a spouse or partner lying next to you, they can't read your mind. It is your thoughts in your brain that you will be alone with. You know whether or not you're confident. You know what it means to be happy or to be satisfied. Give yourself the chance to be as happy as possible by cultivating the right mindset surrounding having confidence.

Life is a journey.

Life is crazy.

Life is unpredictable.

The best tool you can give yourself to prepare for anything that comes your way is to build your confidence. Don't be afraid to be who you are, and remember, at the end of the day, there is nothing wrong with loving yourself.

References

Brown, A. (2019). Types and benefits of exposure therapy. Retrieved from https://www.betterhelp.com/advice/therapy/types-and-benefits-of-exposure-therapy/

Corkindale, G. (2008). Overcoming imposter syndrome. Retrieved from https://hbr.org/2008/05/overcoming-imposter-syndrome

Cuddy, A. (2012). Your body language may shape who you are. Retrieved from https://www.ted.com/talks/amy_cuddy_your_body_language_may_shape_who_you_are?language=en

Fox, M. (2011). Go for your goals and gain confidence. Retrieved from https://www.psychologytoday.com/us/blog/think-confident-be-confident/201106/go-your-goals-and-gain-confidence

Galinsky, A., Hsu, D. Huang, L, Nordgren, D., & Rucker, A. (2014). The music of power: perceptual and behavioral consequences of powerful music. Retrieved from https://journals.sagepub.com/doi/abs/10.1177/1948550614542345

Gilkey, R. & Kilts, C. (2007). Cognitive fitness. Retrieved from https://hbr.org/2007/11/cognitive-fitness

Grohol, J. (2019). 15 common cognitive distortions. Retrieved from https://psychcentral.com/lib/15-common-cognitive-distortions/

Healy, M. (2011). Is self-confidence pre-determined? Retrieved from https://www.psychologytoday.com/us/blog/creative-development/201111/is-self-confidence-pre-determined

Kraft, T. & Pressman, S. (2012). Grin and bear it: The influence of manipulated facial expression on the stress response. Retrieved from

https://journals.sagepub.com/doi/abs/10.1177/0
956797612445312

Lachmann, S. (2013). 10 Sources of Low Self-
Esteem. Retrieved from
https://www.psychologytoday.com/us/blog/me-
we/201312/10-sources-low-self-esteem

Markway, B. (2019). 4 proven approaches to
increase your confidence level. Retrieved from
https://www.psychologytoday.com/intl/blog/shy
ness-is-nice/201810/4-proven-approaches-
increase-your-confidence-level

Newsome, T. (2015). 11 weird signs of low self-
esteem that are easy to miss. Retrieved from
https://www.bustle.com/articles/112199-11-
weird-signs-of-low-self-esteem-that-are-easy-to-
miss

Purcell, M. (2018). The health benefits of
journaling. Retrieved from
https://psychcentral.com/lib/the-health-benefits-
of-journaling/

Randolph, K. (2002). Sports visualizations.
Retrieved from

https://www.llewellyn.com/encyclopedia/article/244

Schacter, D. L., Addis, D. R., Hassabis, D., Martin, V. C., Spreng, R. N., & Szpunar, K. K. (2012). The future of memory: remembering, imagining, and the brain. Neuron, 76(4), 677–694. doi:10.1016/j.neuron.2012.11.001

Scott, E. (2019). 5 emotion-focused coping techniques for stress relief. Retrieved from https://www.verywellmind.com/emotion-focused-coping-for-stress-relief-3145107

Selig, M. (2018). 10 myths about confidence that are holding you back. Retrieved from https://www.psychologytoday.com/us/blog/changepower/201808/10-myths-about-confidence-are-holding-you-back

Thorpe, M. (2017). 12 science-based benefits of meditation. Retrieved from https://www.healthline.com/nutrition/12-benefits-of-meditation

Warnick, M. (2015). 5 kinds of confidence. Retrieved from

https://www.huffpost.com/entry/5-kinds-of-confidence_b_6850918

Whitebourne, S. (2013). The one, most important, way to cope when things go wrong. Retrieved from https://www.psychologytoday.com/us/blog/fulfillment-any-age/201311/the-one-most-important-way-cope-when-things-go-wrong

Wilding, M. (n.d.) 5 different types of imposter syndrome (and 5 ways to battle each one). Retrieved from https://www.themuse.com/advice/5-different-types-of-imposter-syndrome-and-5-ways-to-battle-each-one

Ye, L. (n.d.). 5 psychology-backed exercises that will make you feel more confident. Retrieved from https://blog.hubspot.com/sales/psychology-backed-exercises-more-confident